Trading With Mexico

by

Wallace Thompson

Double9 BOOKS

Trading With Mexico
by Wallace Thompson

ISBN: 978-93-73400-61-7

Published by

DOUBLE 9 BOOKS
2/13-B, Ansari Road
Daryaganj, New Delhi – 110002
info@double9books.com
www.double9books.com
Tel. 011-40042856

ABOUT THE AUTHOR

Wallace Thompson was a writer known for producing analytical works that examined the relationship between economics, politics, and international affairs. With a direct and pragmatic style, Thompson addressed issues of commerce, governance, and foreign relations with clarity and precision. The work was characterized by a strong focus on factual detail and real-world implications, especially in contexts involving trade and diplomacy. Rather than relying on speculation or idealism, Thompson's writing often advocated for practical understanding and cautious engagement, particularly in the realm of international business. The publications reflected a deep awareness of market structures, legal frameworks, and the social dynamics influencing global interaction. Through thoughtful critique and strategic insight, Thompson contributed to a broader understanding of how economic systems operate under political pressures. The approach remained grounded in research and observation, aiming to inform rather than persuade, and offering readers a foundation for navigating complex global relationships. The legacy of the writing lies in its clarity, commitment to accuracy, and relevance to business and policy discussions.

CONTENTS

TO

ALBERT BACON FALL

A Statesman Whose Insight and Whose
Knowledge of Mexico Have Long
Sustained the Faith of Those
Who Love Her Best.

PREFACE

The book whose pages follow is the result of a conviction, firm-rooted in observation and experience, that the American business man prefers to judge for himself. He wishes the facts, and beyond all the fundamental facts, and when he has them his judgment is sure, quick and final. It is to men who think in this way that this book is addressed. It is the story, told as concisely as the facts permit, of conditions as they truly exist in the great land which, like a cornucopia, stretches to the south of us. It is written for the business man of the United States, definitely, with such limitations as exist for such a book—its value to the European may be the greater because it does not seek to straddle the national issue.

I have written other books on Mexico. One has seen the light of publication before this volume was written.[1] I have sought, in these other volumes, one upon the people of Mexico and one upon the psychology which governs their actions in social and in business life, to lay a solid ground for the understanding of the country and its people. In the book which is offered here I give, freely, openly, without apology, the facts of a commercial situation which to me is the most astounding condition in the business world to-day. I picture, with the simplicity of truth, a country of vast natural mineral resources, but virtually no agricultural wealth, a country with almost no consuming population, a country of radical governments which have sought, frankly, to destroy capital and the machinery of Mexico's own wealth. I have told but little of the famous resources of Mexico—those are described elaborately in many works. I have told little of the labor of Mexico, for this is yet to be harnessed. I have described none of the great industrial needs of Mexico, because those are obvious to all who run.

I have sought, rather, to set down those phases of Mexican life to-day which are the background of Mexican business. I have dared—what no man with less faith in the American business man would dare to do—to set forth honestly the truth about Mexicans of to-day, the secrets of Mexican government, the facts of Mexican "bolshevism," the horrors of Mexico's degeneration under the rule of her predatory *caciques*. These to me are the fundamentals of Mexican trade, just as they are the fundamentals of Mexican politics and of the life of the Mexican people to-day. I have sought to set them forth in their relation to the grave issues of world trade, to set them in their relationship with the ways of men in business and with the ways of business in its relationship to human life.

I am a friend of Mexico. Few who have written of her life have been more deeply interested in her welfare. I should like to lay here the foundations for a solution of the Mexican business problem by setting forth the unhappy picture, ignoring no detail, seeking no self-deceit, as is too often the practice of those who write on Mexico. I believe that more will be gained, more business of a solid sort won, by those who realize and recognize the truth of conditions in Mexico, than by those who deliberately close their eyes to those conditions.

Let us have the truth, then! Let us face the Mexican trade problem as it is, with its vast potentialities balanced, as they actually are, by the sinister elements of ignorance, bitter poverty and racial conservatism. Let us see the problem while we see the golden goal. For this problem is no mere issue of beating the British or the Germans to a thriving market. It is an issue of bringing into being the purchasing power of a populous nation, which is bowed down to-day by the horrors of revolution, of unthinking radicalism, of national degeneracy. He who shall solve that problem will win the trade of Mexico when she has trade. That is all which is to be known, and the only issue to be faced.

This book is not a radical document. It does not seek to explain the problems of to-day in terms of to-morrow. The author finds in the radical movements of the present the leaven of the future—little else. He sees in the upheavals of our day a searching for some essential truth which will be a clarifying factor in this time of chaos and distrust. He does not see in them the final solution of any of the difficulties which hatched them out into a too ready world.

Nor is this book reactionary. The author believes that the day of Diaz is long past in Mexico, that the day of the dreamer of utopian visions—Madero—is past in Mexico. He seeks in the present and in the future the sane, firm grasp of actualities which to the watcher on the tower is the only hope of true progress. He sees in the orgies of Carranza and his immediate successors not the upsurgence of mighty ideals, but of personal ambitions and crass disregard of the bases of all human progress. He seeks, in the whirling chaos of the present, a firm footing. He seeks to give the direction of such understanding as he may have to those who think with him. He believes that if he gives such a direction to them, it will enable them to go forward to the winning of some of the vast profits which await them in the Mexican market.

One word more I would add. There rules to-day in Washington a government one of whose mighty maxims is the protection and encouragement of those Americans who to-day go forth, as their fathers went forth before them, to carve their way in the wilderness. The Washington government knows, as we all know, that the only wilderness left to us is the open field of the vast undeveloped lands to the South. I believe that Washington plans definitely to support the American pioneer to the fullest in his new conquest of the New World. That his weapons of conquest are dollars and brains and energy matter not, and that he battles in lands over which the flag shall never fly matters less. The fact that he is an American, that he is honest, that he is patriotic and sincere—these matter much in Washington.

This book, then, goes upon its way, its record clear and envisioned in deep frankness and in deep faith in the American business man and in the American government of to-day. I offer it to those who must go forth, to those who must perforce place the funds at the disposal of those who go, and to those who, in the councils of our government, are quietly, without ostentation or political apology, placing firm hands to the backs of those who dare and who give.

Wallace Thompson.

New York,
August 5, 1921.

FOOTNOTES

[1] *The People of Mexico.* Harper & Bros., New York, 1921. The companion book, *The Mexican Mind,* is in preparation for publication as this present volume goes to press.

CHAPTER I
TRADING WITH MEXICO

Three fundamentals determine and will determine American participation in Mexican trade. Excursions, however wet, will not change those fundamentals. Enthusiasm, however sincere, will not affect them. Above all, promises should not be taken into consideration in our cool judgment of them. American business men have never been noted for sentimentalism in their own country; they should not be sentimental in other countries. Let us take up the situation and look at it with the sane judgment we would apply to the question of selling, say, a new type of water meter in New York City.

The three fundamentals of the Mexican trade question are not unique. They are, first, the Market; second, the Credit, and third, the Government and Laws under which trade must be carried on. Truly not original, and the astonishing thing about American business men who consider Mexico is that they apparently lose sight of them, and most of all lose sight of the emphasis which must be given to each.

First, the Mexican market. Three phases again: the people, the industries and the need. There are 15,000,000 people in Mexico. Of these, 6,000,000 are Indians, and Indians that are comparable, literally, to our own reservation Indians in the United States, in the things they buy and the things they make. There are 8,000,000 mixed-bloods, a cross of Indian and Spanish, but of these 8,000,000 fully 6,000,000 are almost as Indian as their full-blood cousins. In other words, 12,000,000 out of 15,000,000 take and need nothing from the outside world excepting food, at those times, like the present, when they do not produce enough for their own needs. More than that, the money or goods which would pay for imported food for the 12,000,000 are created by the remaining 3,000,000—in other words, the actual market in Mexico is not 15,000,000 people but 3,000,000. The rest wear no shoes—only native tanned sandals. They wear no civilized clothes, only white cotton woven at home. They wear only home-made hats, the raw material the fiber of palm trees which grow wild. They have no need for culture, for houses, for travel. Remember, then, a buying population of 3,000,000.

The industries are limited almost exclusively to the extraction of the riches of the soil by mining and through deep oil wells. In all Mexico, with its vast sweep of territory, virtually nothing is produced for export excepting those riches which come from Mother Earth, and those overwhelmingly under the enterprising management of the foreign companies and individuals who alone have ever sought to develop them. Only one industry in Mexico puts human hands and human brains to the wheel of progress and creates wealth—that is the industry of growing sisal hemp in Yucatan. Sisal hemp is indispensable for the making of binder twine for the world's wheat crop, and is the basis of what was once a great national and international industry. Yet to-day even that commodity has been cut in production almost to the point of destruction, by the machinations of Mexican government and graft, and Yucatan is not to-day the great purchasing center that it once was. Moreover, Yucatan is far from the Mexican mainland, a principality, a country of its own, and its riches have never been a true part of the resources of Mexico, for it buys and sells direct with the outside world.

Gold is the common medium of circulation in Mexico to-day. There is not a peso of Mexican paper currency in use. All is gold, or foreign bills, with low-grade silver and copper as subsidiary coins. The use of gold is reassuring to the business man. It looks like prosperity and it does assure a firm rate of exchange. But the gold in Mexico does not mean these things. Its great significance is the absence of credit. Gold circulates because no man trusts the government, and every piece of gold that passes through your hands in Mexico tells you that Mexico is far from being on a stable financial basis, either as a government or as a business community. Gold is of value, really, only because it makes credit possible. When you must ship boxes of gold into distant states at an appalling rate of insurance against bandits and highwaymen, it is not prosperity, but rather the lack of it. When gold is in circulation, and there are no bills, the available money of the country is limited, literally, to the total of the gold and to not one cent more. When there is paper in circulation it means that the gold supply has been increased many fold because the credit of the government has been added to the gold to supplement the supply of money to be used in trade.

In Mexico there is not only no paper money, but there is practically no commercial paper. The drafts of great foreign companies travel about the land for weeks and months before they are cashed and when they finally reach the bank on which they are drawn, the backs are covered with endorsements, and on some an extra sheet of paper has been pasted to carry more signatures. And that is not good business, and should not be reassuring to the prospective trader.

In Mexico to-day no one trusts the government, and as a result no one trusts his neighbor. The business men of Mexico who are demanding long-term credits abroad will not trust their oldest customers, and cannot themselves get credit in their own country. Recently, when the Mexican government wanted credit on a large supply of railway equipment, it was told that if one young American, engaged in running private trains at heavy cost over the Mexican railway systems, would guarantee the bills, the Mexican government could have what it needed. Otherwise, cash with order. The Mexican government is trying to get railway equipment, and is making promising announcements. But it is getting very little, and for what it is getting it pays almost entirely in cash, or, strangely enough in this age, barters commodities or prepaid freight tickets for it! These are facts, and extremely significant facts. The railway equipment men want to know how the government is going to pay—and that is what all Americans who contemplate trade with Mexico should want to know.

But the need of Mexico, the power we have to help her rehabilitate herself! Ah, that is a strong bid, even with what we have called the unsentimental American business man. He wants to give her a lift now, when she needs it, and then he will not be forgotten when the big splitting up of profits comes. Perhaps this is true. Let us look at it. For some years now we have been following the very laudable and beautiful system of going more than half way with Mexico. We are still urged to follow this excellent method. The only trouble is that the "more than half way" is getting longer and longer, and Mexico is asking more and more and giving less and less. The kindly souls who have sought to get into Mexico with their surplus stocks are not gaining anything, except curses and distrust. So far, save for the promises which have always been forthcoming, there is nothing coming out of Mexico to help the trade we are hearing about.

Most of the talk about Mexican trade for American manufacturers was born, moreover, of our own need to get rid of accumulated goods. Beginning late in 1919, there was considerable inflow of these cheap goods into Mexico on good terms. Those who were fortunate enough to unload talked of it, and the gossip went about that Mexico was a fine place to sell off extra stocks. But after a year, the unloading system began to glut the Mexican market, and to-day, when the same manufacturers want to sell again, they find that Mexico will take—only goods at sacrifice prices. They went half way and more, did our manufacturers, and Mexico did not "come back." Instead she sat tight where we came to her, and insisted on our coming a little further with concessions to her needs and wants. The result is that to-day there is nothing like the demand for American goods that there was when we first did the unloading which we thought would whet the Mexican appetite. Mexico is like the customer of a "fire sale" store—she will buy only the most obvious bargains. It is cash trade for a section of a town where there used to be credit, and where there is no credit to-day. But the customer is again demanding credit—and cash-trade bargains at the same time.

This question of credit is of necessity complicated. But perhaps the answer as far as the American business man is concerned is contained in the fact that while the Mexican merchant demands credit he himself does not give credit—no country was ever on so thorough a cash basis as Mexico is to-day. The merchant who is asking for credit is carrying on his business from hand to mouth; he has no accounts on his books to guarantee the goods for which he is promising to pay. He asks credit on his character standing and on the possibilities of his market—he offers literally nothing else. Personally, many Mexicans and many foreigners in Mexico are reliable and honest men, but no sane business man would take in the United States risks similar to those demanded by his prospective customers in Mexico. And the possibilities of the market—those are as yet thin air and enthusiastic hope, which gain strength only from our national need to get a foreign outlet to keep our plants going. Let the American manufacturer weigh these two considerations with the additional realization that there is no reserve credit in the background.

Reserve credit, such as bills payable, sound real estate values and prospects of peace and good business years ahead, are comparable to the unseen sources of energy in the human body, on which that body lives and thrives during lean periods. Mexico's lean period has now lasted for eleven long years, and in that period the country has been living literally on its reserves alone. Again and again one hears the expression, "Mexico is living on her fat," and the continued marvel is that she has lived so long and survived such lengthened calamities through so many ghastly years of destruction. As this is written, there has been some appearance of regeneration, a noisily announced period of "reconstruction." But as yet this is only an appearance. Actually while the wheels of business and life are running more smoothly for the moment, this is obviously a surface condition—deep down under the surface of Mexican life the wasted tissue remains. Mexico is not yet filling the interstices of her flesh with that reserve strength which is business credit and business promise.

But why not help in the rebuilding, and thus take a risk which will probably bring great gain in the years of progress to come?

The answer to this question must be based on a thorough understanding of the third of our three great issues—Mexican Government and Law as applied to business. The Mexican revolutions which began in 1910 had for their announced object, "Mexico for the Mexicans." The idea was to bring the foreigner under control of Mexican law and government. This was eminently just—if it were true, as assumed, that under the Diaz régime the foreigners had been above the Mexican law. The facts were largely otherwise, however, despite some glaring abuses. In the working out of the idea of "Mexico for the Mexicans," the revised as well as the entirely new legislation and procedure went far beyond the normal reaction against the alleged irregularities of the Diaz time.

In the new "Constitution of 1917," which is literally the most radical written constitution of any country in the world to-day, the chief, if not the only object was to make difficult the operation of foreigners in any line of business in the country. The laws against their holding land are drastic and final in their import; no foreigner may own property within sixty miles of the border or within thirty miles of the sea; foreigners may not control a Mexican corporation formed for the purpose of holding such land unless they waive their citizenship rights with respect to such companies; great estates are prohibited, so that true agricultural industry is made virtually impossible; foreign plans for irrigation projects—the one hope of the Mexican farmer—are nipped and killed; most serious of all, such lands are virtually confiscated through nationalization projects which have already been applied to many great properties, some of them of foreigners, and have been kept from affecting others only by active diplomatic protest.

But, the casual observer of things Mexican asks, how is it that business still continues? How is it that the oil companies to whom, we are told, these nationalization laws especially apply, how is it that the oil companies are still doing business, are still drilling wells and taking out oil? Does this not mean that these laws are merely provisions against a revival of the abuses of the old days? These are the questions that occur, as the Mexicans planned them to occur, to the outside observer.

The Mexicans assure us that this is truly the case, but the effect of the laws is very different. Their effect is to place all business, Mexican and American, foreign oil wells and native merchants alike, in the status of receiving the *privilege* of doing business, in place of the *right* of doing business. In effect they make every foreigner in Mexico, from the missionaries who conduct services contrary to the law of the land which prohibits foreigners from officiating as priests before their own altars to the oil men who dig wells under permits wheedled out of a grasping government department, law-breakers or receivers of special and "pernicious" privilege. To-day no business man can defend his rights before the courts of Mexico, for all rights, even the common rights of corporate business, are in some way or another contradictory to the laws of the land. They receive privilege, and privilege in great and generous measure—if they are friendly to the ruling group or their satellites. They receive privilege by the grace of government, not rights by the power of government. Government theoretically exists for the protection of the weak, but government in Mexico exists actually for the exploitation of the strong by officials and for the suppression of the weak if the strong want and can pay for such suppression.

Strangely enough, the strong in Mexico are not altogether contented with this condition. Somehow business, with its awakening consciousness to its helplessness, is finding the situation irksome. The greatest single industry in Mexico to-day is oil, and oil pays about $50,000,000 a year in various taxes to the Mexican government—and for what? Almost all of it for the privilege of doing business, and the result is that oil is at the mercy, to-day, of government caprice and the caprice of Mexican officials. The laws of the present era of Mexico are enacted literally for the purpose of having a "club" of control over all forms of business activity, laws to be enforced when it is convenient, or to be "forgotten" when that is desirable. The oil companies spend time and vast effort to keep their protests to the Washington and Mexican governments in good order—so that the price of their privileges may be kept low. The legitimate portion of their taxes is only about forty per cent of the total sum they pay, but it is probably literally true that they would pay all they now pay and more if they could dispense with the rule of privilege and trade it for decent human rights to do decent business in a decently governed country.

In this, these companies are fighting the fight of the individual business man as well as the fight of their own stockholders. It may all be selfish, and doubtless is, but by a strange turn of affairs, the laws of Mexico have worked out to the creation of salable privilege instead of defensible rights, and this has thrown all business into the same group. The business problem of Mexico is literally the achievement of this exchange of privileges for rights. And until that exchange is effected, he is but a gambler who goes into Mexico to seek or to offer honest business, for even though he should gain much sure profit in the beginning, those profits will be more than wiped out later unless the legitimate business of Mexico is given the legitimate rights of business.

And how is this exchange of privileges for rights to be effected? This is the problem that confronts American business and American government to-day. The issue is joined clean and is simple indeed. The provisions of the Mexican Constitution of 1917 and the laws which give it effect remain on the Mexican statute books to-day because they are profitable to the group in control of the government. They mean, literally, graft and power, for where privilege is necessary for the carrying out of business, there is a price on privilege, but where rights are provided for business, the price and the prize are upon industry and activity.

To the members of the American Chambers of Commerce on tour in Mexico, to the American manufacturers who are invited to ship goods to Mexico to-day, offers of privilege are made, privilege without graft or price, now. But the price is there, and is clearly worked out in the subtle Mexican mind. These American business men, pleased with their reception, are to become boosters of the Mexican government, demanding its recognition and scouting the great financial interests who are their traditional enemies at home. That is price enough to the Mexican mind. But when recognition is gained, and when those same individuals seek to do business in Mexico under "normal" conditions, the laws which ensconce privilege and give it into the hands of petty and high officials for dispensation, will reap their toll.

One way only remains—the removal of privilege, the establishment of rights. Insistence on these issues alone will almost solve the Mexican problems politically and commercially. But the Mexicans are wise indeed when they seek to divide the counsels of this country, to place the small American business man and manufacturer in a position of antagonism to the issues that are set clear in Washington, the issues of political privilege versus political rights, the issues of the business privileges which those individual Americans seek to gain for themselves versus the business rights that will include them and all their fellows.

The call is again for clear foresight and not for sentimentalism, for a social conception of business and not for a selfish, individualistic hope of getting in ahead of the next fellow. The Americans who have been longest in Mexico are begging to-day for rights in exchange for privilege. They know, as those who look upon Mexico from outside or as newcomers do not know, that until Mexico mends her ways with business, business can never rescue Mexico from the slough of her present unhappiness. They know that no business in any nation can long prosper without the prosperity and the good sense of the government of that nation. They are not pirates, and they know that piracy, in government or in business, leads but to the destruction of both. What they know we may have for the listening. If we do not take it, we, too, must learn, as they learned, in the costly school of experience.

CHAPTER II NATURE AND THE MEXICAN MARKET[2]

Every land upon this globe owes to nature that predetermination of its products and its needs which are the vital factors of its commerce and its industries. Even the nature of its races, which has so much to do with the standards of living which affect the quality and volume of business, is determined to a certain extent by climate and geography. It is therefore a fundamental need of all who have a deep interest in Mexican business to grasp something of the location, the formation, and the climate of that country. For few nations in the world have a more wonderful location, and few have a more disastrous climate.

The vast cornucopia-like triangle of land which comprises the territory of Mexico lies south of nearly three-quarters of the southern boundary of the United States. Its western tip touches Southern California at the Pacific and its most easterly point is 500 miles south of the Pensacola, at the western end of Florida. For 1,833 miles Mexico's northern border is contiguous to the United States, 693 miles eastward along arbitrarily marked lines from the Pacific Ocean to El Paso, Texas, and the remainder southeastward along the sinuous course of the Rio Grande to the Gulf of Mexico. Its jagged southern border is hardly 400 miles long, touching Guatemala and British Honduras (Belize).

This cornucopia, grasping the Gulf of Mexico on the east like a great hand, swings southeastward from the Pacific contact with the United States until the most westerly point of the Guatemalan border is 500 miles *east* of Mexico's easternmost contact with the United States on the north.

Set apart, as Mexico is by her boundaries, she seems in form much like a great peninsula, but she has, herself, two important peninsulas as part of her territorial extent and configuration. One is the Peninsula of Yucatan, which forms the eastern end of the cornucopia, the thumb of the curving hand which grasps the Gulf of Mexico, an area of about 50,000 square miles. The other is the long, narrow peninsula of Lower California, with 58,343 square miles, extending directly south of the American state of California and connected with the Mexican mainland by only a narrow strip.

That mainland comprises, with the two peninsulas, 765,762 square miles, and the 1,561 square miles of coastal islands under Mexican sovereignty bring the total area of the country up to 767,323 square miles. The greatest width of the mainland is 750 miles, and the greatest length is 1,942 miles, from the northwestern tip of Lower California, where it joins the United States, to the southernmost point in the jagged Guatemalan border in the Mexican state of Chiapas. The narrowest point in Mexico is 120 miles, at the Isthmus of Tehuantepec, once discussed as the possible site of an interoceanic canal, and in the time of Diaz the route of a great transshipping railway between the Pacific and the Gulf of Mexico. The Atlantic (Gulf of Mexico) coastline of Mexico is 1,727 miles long, that of the Pacific (including the long border of Lower California) 4,574 miles.

Lying between 32° 30′ and 14° 30′ North Latitude and 86° 30′ to 117° Longitude west from Greenwich, the triangular form of the Mexican territory places it about equally in the temperate and torrid zones. This is a primary factor in Mexican climate, but far more significant is the contour of the country itself.

This is largely mountainous, for if we include the high but fertile table-lands, nearly two-thirds of the country is covered with mountain ranges. The Rocky Mountains of the United States, the great backbone of the Western Hemisphere, cross the Mexican border into Sonora, in a low, narrow range. Almost immediately south of the international line they begin spreading eastward. A long, slowly rising valley a hundred miles wide continues southward from El Paso, narrowing rapidly, while to the eastward of this valley rises an apparently new range of mountains, obviously a part of the great Rocky Mountain range, but unconnected with it in the United States and south, indeed, of the broad flat plains of Texas. This is the *Sierra Madre Oriental*, or Eastern Mother Range, the continuation of the Rockies in Sonora and Durango being called the *Sierra Madre Occidental*, or Western Mother Range. Further south, these two join together, and spread to virtually the whole width of Mexico, excepting for the Gulf coastal plain, some 300 miles wide, to the east. All of Central Mexico is mountainous, flattened only by vast plateaus which, according to the accepted geological theory, were created by alluvial deposits and lava dust from the mountains which rise still above them. At the Isthmus of Tehuantepec, the Sierra Madre flattens out till, save for the relatively easy grades which climb from the Gulf and from the Pacific to the summit of the low divide (less than 300 feet above sea level) the mountains might be all but gone. The narrow plane of the Isthmus passed, the mountains rise again until the center of the state of Chiapas is once more a vast plateau accented with towering peaks, a formation which continues southward through Central America, lowers again at Panama, but joins directly, at last, with the South American Andes.

In this sweep of mountainous territory are hundreds of deep cañons or *barrancas,* great fertile plateaus, and many wonderful mountains. Of these last those about the Valley of Anahuac, the site of Mexico City and for ages the center of Mexican government and population, are the most famous. Here are Popocatepetl (17,520 feet) and Ixtaccihuatl (16,960 feet) the snow-peaked volcanoes, and to the eastward the still more beautiful cone of Orizaba (18,250 feet). Virtually at the same latitude, but far to the west, is Colima, (12,991 feet), a still active volcano. Toluca (14,950 feet), close to the Valley of Mexico, Malinche (14,636 feet) in the state Tlaxcala, the Cofre de Perote (13,400 feet) in the state of Vera Cruz, and Tancitaro (12,664 feet) are those of greatest height. Only the already great altitude of the plateaus of Mexico from which most of the striking mountains spring keeps hundreds of others from filling the eye of the traveler. The scenery which results from the mountainous formations of Mexico is literally unsurpassed, for Popocatepetl and Ixtaccihuatl can give the climber all the thrills of the Alps, and the crater lakes to be found in one or two sections of Mexico rival in splendor the more famous resorts in Europe.

The deep and wide *barrancas* which mark the mountainous formation all through Mexico are magnificent to contemplate, but the day's journey down and up the sides of such a geological spectacle as the Barranca of Beltran brings home to even the unscientific observer the terrific handicaps which these vast cuts put upon the industrial development of the country. Much of the conquering of these handicaps was achieved under the broad railway policy of President Diaz, and the work done still remains, but many years must now pass before the final conquest is achieved. Such a work as the building of the Colima branch of the Mexican Central, completing the only direct line for the first time from the Capital to the Pacific, will hardly be repeated when revolution threatens, for here, in less than 100 miles, twenty great bridges had to be built, most of them crossing *barrancas* and cuts of mere geological formation, with virtually no streams filling them even in the rainy season. The Southern Pacific line from the northern border in Sonora lacks but sixty miles of linking up with the Guadalajara branch of the National Railways, but thirty of those sixty miles are through a mountainous territory cut with deep *barrancas* which will cost close to a million dollars a mile to build.

Such *barrancas* and valleys do not, of themselves, indicate either great natural water power or navigable streams. There are wonderful water power possibilities in Mexico, to be sure, which come from two factors, the sheer drops which give ideal power sites with tremendous heads of water, and the heavy torrential rainy season. But the streams themselves do not carry sufficient water the year round to justify any plant, and tremendous reservoir development is vital to any power plant design. Such reservoirs have been built in various parts of Mexico, but at appalling expense, such as only great financial interests can swing—only foreign capital or the government has been able to handle them. There is an added and unexpected element of difficulty—the porousness of much of the soil of Mexico. The mountains, indeed, are of igneous rocks, but underneath the valleys is often soft limestone, and more often still, under those places where a great impounding of water might be made with a relatively low and inexpensive dam, is the soft, porous alluvial and volcanic-ash land with which the valleys have been filled up.

This porous soil and limestone are factors bearing on the absence of navigable streams. Even in the lowlands the streams run underground in Mexico, and while they can be tapped by shallow wells, they deprive Mexico almost entirely of the advantages of river transportation. Even the Rio Grande, on the northern border, is useless for navigation most of the year. The Panuco, at whose mouth is located the great oil center of Tampico, is navigable only a short distance above that port. The broad, rich coastal plain along the Gulf of Mexico is watered by tiny streams, all of which, excepting the partially navigable Papaloapam, are useless for steamers and even for launches most of the year. Not until we reach the Isthmus of Tehuantepec do we find a river worth considering for transportation. The Coatzacoalcos, at whose mouth on the Gulf of Mexico is Puerto Mexico (the eastern terminus of the Tehuantepec National Railway), furnishes a highway which made possible the relatively great development of American tropical plantations during the years of peace under Diaz. Its mouth was then the port of loading for great ships, but only by continual dredging was it kept open, and to-day the port is abandoned except for light-draft coasting ships. Further south, emptying into the Gulf at Frontera, is the magnificent system of which the Grijalva and the Usumacinta are the chief streams. Here indeed have plied and in the future will ply great river steamers, for upon the banks of the Usumacinta, at least, are rich oil fields and the fairest farming land in all tropical Mexico. Both the Grijalva and the Usumacinta are magnificent streams, and the latter is comparable, in its majestic volume, to the Mississippi itself. Only the bar at Frontera keeps them from being navigable to ocean steamers. For a brief period under President Madero this bar was dredged so that fruit boats could enter and go to the docks of banana farms, encouraging a promising industry which was killed by heavy taxation and government neglect of the dredging, under the revolutionary presidents of recent years. But this one system of rivers offers virtually all there is of navigation in Mexico.

Yucatan, the peninsula which separates the Caribbean sea from the Gulf of Mexico, is virtually without rivers, the water from the abundant rainfall of its interior finding its way to underground streams in the porous underlying coral limestone.

On the west coast there are a few rivers. The most important is the Lerma, which waters a large territory on the Pacific side of the continental divide, and allows some local transportation. The Balsas, in the states of Oaxaca and Guerrero, reaches far inland, but rapids and shallows make its use for navigation expensive and all but impossible. In Sonora is the Yaqui river, navigable for small boats and of some value for transportation. The Fuerte is also in this class.

Another phase of the geography of Mexico which affects transportation is the complete absence of good natural harbors well located. The chief port of Mexico, Vera Cruz, has a harbor which was built artificially around a partially protected bay. Tampico is a port solely because of the jetties which narrow the mouth of the Panuco and, with the help of dredges, keep the channel clear. Puerto Mexico has a similar problem, but the smaller river makes dredging absolutely vital. Frontera is solely a dredging proposition, as the Usumacinta and the Grijalva, emptying together into the Gulf, have formed a vast delta in the lowlands which can probably never be narrowed to take advantage of the great volume of water which they pour out. Yucatan has literally no semblance of a harbor, and its great crops of sisal hemp are loaded from lighters at appalling expense.

On the Pacific coast, Acapulco has one of the ideal harbors of the world, completely landlocked, and open for medium-draft ships. But it is relatively small, and moreover as yet almost inaccessible to any railway survey, although it was used by the galleons from Manila as a port for transshipment of the treasures of the Orient across Mexico to the galleons from Cadiz which came to Vera Cruz. Salina Cruz, the Pacific terminus of the Tehuantepec National Railway, was built from an open roadstead with two lines of jetties and seawalls, a work which inattention has now all but ruined. Manzanillo, the terminus of the only direct railway line from Mexico City to the Pacific, was also built with seawalls and opened by dredges. Mazatlan, further up the coast, and the chief port of the Southern Pacific Railway of Mexico, is an open roadstead. Guaymas, the port of the state of Sonora, is accessible only to light-draft ships.

These are all great natural handicaps, and have affected the life of Mexico probably more than it will be possible to estimate. The mighty and costly work of the Diaz régime in building harbors is a monument to that "materialistic" era which will last through many years and has already played a tremendous part in furnishing the sinews of revolution to succeeding governments, for without that work Mexico would be far from capable of sustaining herself in the period of her agony to-day.

But beyond all these factors of mountains and rivers and sea looms a yet greater problem, and still more far-reaching—the problem of climate. As noted, Mexico lies in about equal parts in the temperate and torrid zones. But the geological zones are far more important, for climate is affected not alone by latitude but by altitude as well. These geological zones are three, the hot country or *tierra caliente*, the temperate country or *tierra templada* and the (relatively) cold country or *tierra fria*. The hot country is the lowland section along the coasts from sea level to 3,000 feet altitude, where the mean annual temperature varies from 76° to 88° Fahrenheit. The Mexican terminology includes not only the lowlands of the torrid zone, but the whole coastal plain up to the northern border. The *tierra templada* lies along the mountain slopes and in the lower plateaus, between 3,000 and 6,500 feet altitude, where the temperature is between 65° and 76°. This zone takes in the higher northern sections which are within the temperate zone proper. The *tierra fria* takes in the high plateaus and the mountains, between 6,500 and 12,500 feet, the yearly average temperatures varying from 30° to 60°, although the important sections record 50° or more. The three geological zones each include about equal portions of the country, but half of the inhabitants live in the cold zone, and only a quarter each in the temperate and hot sections. The mean temperatures of the cold zone are approximately those recognized as the most favorable for physical exertion, but in the hot country the body struggles against a handicap of almost 20° F. more than the 65° at which it normally functions best. More significant still are the temperatures of all the zones in their relation to mental activity. The human mind is at its best under the stimulus of a mean temperature of about 40° F., but even at Mexico City, 7,600 feet above sea level, the mean temperature of winter is as high as 53°. In the temperate and hot countries the handicaps under which the brain functions run to 20° and up to 45° above the 40° at which the human mind works at highest efficiency. No stimulating winters, no clarifying cool spells, even, in the midst of the endlessly beautiful summers of Mexico!

Only the cold zone has any advantages in temperature, and these advantages are equally important with the fertility of the soil in accounting for the predominance of population there. Yet even where the temperature is favorable to at least physical work, there is the debilitating sameness of the tropics, the assurance that there will always be more difference between day and night than between the seasons. There, on the heights, too, the nervous drain of altitude and of lack of moisture in the air takes the place—with no advantage to the human machine—of the humidity and heat of the hot country. At every turn in Mexico climate takes toll of human energy, even if we ignore the undoubtedly debilitating effect of tropical and sub-tropical light upon the white men and upon their mixed-blood descendants as well.

All these climatic factors, then, have continuous influence on the health of all the Mexican people as well as upon Mexican business. The hot, humid weather of the hot country makes those who live there low in resistance of disease, while the nervous strain of the altitudes and dryness of air in the better portions achieves a not dissimilar result in lowering resistance. It is axiomatic that the Mexicans as a people are seldom well and, as has been recorded in detail elsewhere,[3] this ill-health has been and is to-day one of the determinants of the relatively low state of progress of the country. No people who are continually sick and upon whose energies their climate is a continuous drain can work well or achieve greatly.

The relation of this thoroughly recognized factor of ill-health to Mexican trade and commerce must not be overlooked. It is at the root of much of the apathy which keeps the Mexican people at their low ebb of business enterprise. It determines with peculiar insistence their predilection for the easy road, the "*mañana* habit," even for the dominance of outworn traditional methods in agriculture and in business. It has a great deal to do with the ease with which foreigners develop a land which has for centuries lain virtually fallow. But it places vast difficulties in the way of that development, for it keeps the labor problem continually in the foreground and vitiates much of the great advantage which the relative cheapness of that labor seems to offer. It has and will continue to have a powerful effect on trade, for it keeps even the enterprising among Mexican business men at a low standard of efficiency and makes it almost imperative that foreigners, for the present, do most of the jobbing and export and much of the retail trade and export buying of the country. This element is too likely to be lost sight of, because it is not a condition common to other lands. But it explains much that seems at first inexplicable in the difficulties of the American exporter and importer in getting the adequate representation in Mexico which he must have.

Another vitally important effect of Mexican geography is the uncertainty and untoward distribution of rainfall. This has forced upon the Mexicans their diet of corn and with it their use of fiery condiments which are probable causes of the digestive disorders which ravage all classes. Moreover, the rainfall conditions have been vitally important in the determination of the entire agricultural tendency of the country.

The seasons in Mexico are marked, not by winter cold and summer heat so much as by seasons of rain and drought. The winter is the dry season, roughly between October and May, and the summer is the salubrious rainy season, from June to September. The distribution of rain throughout the year and the failure of the rains in the important growing seasons in some of the otherwise fertile sections is due primarily to the geography of the country. Professor Ellsworth Huntington, of Yale, the great American climatologist, finds that Mexico's summer rains are due to the vertical rays of the sun which cause the rapid rising of the heated air, with sudden expansion and condensation, first over the low-lying hot country and later on the rising uplands of the *tierra templada*, where the function of the mountains in bringing about condensation is amply proven by the well-watered eastern slopes and the dry western sides of the ranges.

This mountain contour and the peculiar shape of the Mexican mainland (very wide at the north in proportion to the south) create another important climatological effect—the broad stretches of desert in the northern sections. The so-called continental type of climate which forms the American deserts further north combines with the mountain contour and the distance from the eastern seashore (driving the rain-clouds southward) to make immense sections of Mexico desert, capable of supporting, at best, only wandering herds. These deserts lie between the broad arms of the great "Y" of the Mexican mountain ranges, and combined with the mountainsides themselves render nearly three-fourths of the area of Mexico unfit for cultivation, even if irrigation were general.

The result is that of the 500,000,000 acres of land in Mexico, not more than 25,000,000 acres are arable. Great sections are useless, so that in the state of Chihuahua, 90,000 square miles in extent, only about 125,000 acres, or less than two-tenths of one per cent can be cultivated—and most of that arable portion is irrigated.

The most fertile sections of Mexico are rich indeed, and in the plateau valleys, where alluvial deposits and lava dust have been poured in together to form the soil, great crops can be raised—when there is rain. Only in a relatively limited section, however, is rain sure to come at the times needed by the crops. Often when it does come, it is in torrential downpours which are likely to wash cultivated fields away in a single night. It is this condition which makes the so-called *tierra templada*, on the slopes of the mountains, in many ways the least desirable of all the farming land of Mexico.

Uncertainty of rainfall is, then, one of the outstanding results of the Mexican climate as influenced by Mexican geography. This uncertainty works forever upon the mind of the Mexican farmer, making him a hopeless fatalist, making it less than worth his while to attempt scientific cultivation. If there is rain, his crops are good anyway, and if there is not rain, the cost of labor and fertilizer and good seed are lost. The Mexican farmer is the worst of gamblers, and his fondest hope is that his average crop over a period of years will be twenty-five per cent of normal!

Famine has ravaged Mexico periodically for thousands of years. It is most interesting, in looking at the present stage (when the largest items of import are foodstuffs), to realize that it has probably been only the much-abused hacienda system which has saved Mexico from severe ravages of recent famine. The hacienda system, which is the operation of huge estates under an elaborate overseership, approaches as nearly as the living conditions of the country permit to a businesslike administration of the farming of the land. It was the stable factor in Mexican food production in the time of the Spaniards and in the later era of Diaz.

The small farmer of Mexico has worked, since the beginning of Indian history, without a thought of supplying the market and thus feeding the industrial workers of the towns. He has lived from hand to mouth, and only when he chances to have a surplus does he transport it or sell it on the ground for the needs of the city market. So true is this that in the period of mining and industrial expansion under Diaz, the draining of the labor from the haciendas to the mines and to the few factories had an immediate effect on the food production, and the imports of foreign corn and wheat grew almost in exact proportion to the diversion of this labor to industry. The small farmers, the Indians and peons, who had places of their own or worked in the village commons, did not go to the mines, but continued their relatively easy existence on their own little *fincas*. They learned only slowly the possibilities of the increased market for their product, and only to an infinitesimal degree did they rise to meet that market.

To-day, with the shutting down of hundreds of the haciendas, and the return of the country to its primeval agriculture, the situation has become extremely serious, and the food importations have grown out of all proportion to the industrial growth of the country; in fact, almost in inverse ratio to the industrial depression of the country.

This presents a serious problem, but it also presents a promise of new opportunity when peace comes to Mexico. For then there must come a revival of large-scale farming, the growth of a new farming system, and with it a tremendously increased market for modern farm implements. There has been much talk, on the part of the revolutionary governments, of the needs of the new small farmers for agricultural machinery, but this is almost entirely talk, for the new small farmers are only falling back to the way of their ancestors, and are not in any sense taking the place of the ruined haciendas in food production for the cities and industrial sections. That development will probably come in the form of an entirely new system of agriculture, in which foreign machinery and of necessity foreign capital must have a vital part.

One of the inevitable developments of Mexican agriculture must be in the direction of irrigation. There is literally not enough good accessible land which will produce without irrigation to feed the country or, what is more important, to make an increase of population possible. This land must be created by irrigation, and irrigation, owing to the geographical formation of the country, must of necessity be carried out by great capital. Many of the village communes have irrigation systems, of a crude sort. Water is brought from distant streams, where it flows after the rainy season, and in some places it is brought up from the underground streams by means of crude water-wheels operated by man-power. But the total area watered by such irrigation is relatively insignificant, and as dams can be built in Mexico only at large cost, the true development of Mexican irrigation waits on peace, on foreign capital and government investment and encouragement.

Something of this sort had been begun before the present era of revolutions. In the closing years of the Diaz régime (before 1911) many franchises were granted to large private companies which planned irrigation projects, and the sum of 90,000,000 pesos was ordered expended on government irrigation over a period of years. A few of the private companies had put their plans into execution, and many others, on the way to accomplishment, were nipped and destroyed by the subsequent revolutions. For the past ten years, nothing has been done toward solving the problems of irrigating the fertile but unwatered lands of Mexico, and it seems hardly likely that anything will be done under the threats of confiscation which now hang over all great enterprise there.

Rainfall conditions have had much to do with the overemphasis on the land problem and indeed with the failure of succeeding governments to solve that problem. As in all arid countries, water rights were originally more important to the natives than were land rights. In hundreds of the Indian communes which still persist, the communal rights of the Indians are distributed, not on the basis of land assigned, but of the water allowed; each Indian receives a proportion of the water brought by the communal irrigation ditches, and may take three or four times the amount of land which his water will irrigate—for crop rotation, forage, etc. This inevitable emphasis on water has perhaps had its part in directing the attention of the Indians in their demands for land distribution, toward the cultivated haciendas where water is available. But it also gives promise for a future which will make possible the rehabilitation of the country through great irrigation projects creating thousands of rich small tracts available for distribution to industrious natives—and foreign small farmers as well. In the government franchises given under Diaz to private irrigation projects, provision was made that about one-third of the land brought into cultivation should be turned over to the government for distribution to small native farmers.

Aside from the indirect effect of these rainfall conditions, they have determined, with imperative insistence, the type of agriculture which is followed in Mexico, and so have affected her trade in foods and raw materials. They have made corn (maize) the staple food of the country, as wheat is the staple of the lands where there is winter snow and regular rainfall throughout the year. They have allowed the development of only the tropical products like coffee, sugar and rubber in the rich districts of Vera Cruz and Oaxaca which were partially opened by foreign stock companies under Diaz. They have, more than all, enthroned, as the only important agricultural export of Mexico, the sisal hemp of Yucatan. This desert product, which requires slow growth for the maturing of the long stout fibers which make rope and binder twine, is the greatest export of Mexico which is the product of Nature's bounty and human enterprise. Coffee and some rubber and tobacco and a little sugar were raised for export in happier days, but only sisal hemp, the product of the desert *henequen* plant, has become a wealth-producer in any great quantity. Mexico has long been an importer of foodstuffs, for, as I have noted, before the days of modern commerce, famine came with terrible regularity. Under Diaz, food was imported in increasing quantities, and since his fall, Mexico has been utterly dependent on the outside world for a large portion of the nutriment of her people.

It is impossible now to predict when and how Mexico will become an agricultural country in fact as well as in potentialities. Irrigation must come, for only when it does will agriculture and the prosperity of agriculture fill the land. In one section where irrigation has been carried out on a large scale—the Laguna district near Torreon, Coah.—cotton is grown in quantity. This product feeds into the native industry of cotton weaving which flourishes near Orizaba and in other sections where local, direct water-power is available.

It seems inevitable that the increase in irrigated lands will add to the acreage of cotton and also to the number and importance of agricultural products of the class of raw materials. The country which irrigation will water in Mexico is of vast extent, and is safely comparable, even at its worst, with what the lands of Utah and California and the Imperial Valley were before water was brought to them. Again, however, we wait on peace and on the great works of modern scientific irrigation. And, however enthusiastic we may be as tradesmen, our capital will not be rushing to seek Mexican investments of this sort until civilized government again rules, with a promise of relative permanency.

The desert character of the country in the north was responsible for the establishment of a great cattle-raising industry, for the land was cheap and the ranges were vast. This has to-day been virtually wiped out, and Mexico imports meat from the United States—all the result of revolution, so that when peace comes the cattle industry will surely be revived. But always the cattle of northern Mexico have been of the range, still unfit for profitable slaughter, and sections suitable for their fattening have been badly needed. There was, in other days, much shipment of range cattle into the United States, and to the better watered southern sections of Mexico. But although peace will bring a revival of the ranges, Mexico cannot look forward to becoming a great meat-producing country until the irrigation problem is solved.

There are rich, well-watered sections of Mexico—this must not be overlooked—but these have resulted in a crowding of population on the plateaus and through the rich valleys such as that of the Lerma river in Jalisco state, and have contributed but little toward the broad development of the country. In fact, one of the characteristics of Mexico's population distribution has been the tendency to gather into groups, so that a great city like the capital or like Guadalajara or Puebla will have a dozen cities and villages of considerable size close about it—and then stretches of sparsely populated country for leagues until another group is found. This is essentially climatic—and geographical.

The mountain contour of the country and this same grouping of the important centers of population have been the chief influences in the location of the railways. Owing to the absence of navigable streams, the mere possibility of Mexico's industrial and of even her true national development had to wait upon the coming of the railways. The first line was that completed in 1872 by English capital between Vera Cruz, the chief port of the Gulf of Mexico, and the City of Mexico, some 400 miles inland and a mile and a half above the level of the port. This "Mexican Railway" touches the groups of cities along the old Spanish highway, and gave them an industrial primacy which was unchallenged until the very last years of the Diaz peace.

After the building of this first line railway construction turned to follow the great natural avenues laid out by the mountain valleys. There were, as we have seen, two main valleys, that between the Eastern and Western Mother ranges, and that to the east of the Eastern chain. Looking at a map of Mexico, the most casual observer is struck by the fact mentioned more than once by Mexican revolutionists, that both these valleys lead directly to the heart of the United States. The railroads which were built there might indeed be taken to have been built to drain Mexico's resources into the United States. But it was only because these roadbeds had been laid out by Nature herself that the lines came to be built there, with the inevitable result of increasing immeasurably the importance of the United States to Mexican development. One early Mexican president (Sebastian Lerdo de Tejada, 1872-76), in fact, refused to allow these obvious roads to be built, explaining, in a much-quoted phrase: "Between the weak and the strong, let the desert remain."

The roads were both built by American companies under President Diaz, the Mexican National on the east, the Mexican Central on the west. They had a mighty part to play in the modernizing of Mexico, and in her development through the trade in the minerals and in the building of such industries as followed them. Throughout their history to the present, they have been of far greater importance to Mexico than to her allegedly covetous northern neighbor.

After these lines were built, others came, to follow the mountain valleys. One went from Mexico City westward to Guadalajara, tapping the rich Valley of the Lerma, the granary of Mexico. Narrow gauge lines twisted through the rich states of Mexico and Michoacan, lines which when modernized and extended in some future time will open agricultural and mining territory comparable to anything yet known to commerce and Mexican industry. Another line found its way to Oaxaca, deep in the mountains to the east and south of Mexico City. Others followed the seacoast to the Isthmus of Tehuantepec, and crossed that narrow, shallow neck of land to the Pacific.

Along the western slope of the Sierra Madre other lines were built through Sonora, and then the Southern Pacific of Mexico, an American company, pushed these roads still further southward, opening new territory, not to the commerce of Central Mexico, but to that of the United States. And last of all, the line to Guadalajara left its easy grades and smooth roadbed to leap the *barrancas* and climb down the mountains to achieve the contact with the Pacific at Manzanillo. A mighty hand, indeed, has nature had in the locating of Mexico's railway lines, and with their connection to the United States and our trade.

The mountainous character of the Mexican territory has upturned vast mineral resources, whose effect on the development of the country has been greater perhaps than any other single fact. These minerals gave the wealth of the Aztecs which tempted the Spaniards to take and to develop the country so thoroughly. They were drained for the three centuries that Spain ruled, and their exploitation shaped all the policy of the colonial régime. They were the greatest of the attractions to foreign capital at the beginning of the Diaz rule, and they paid most of the revenue of taxes upon which the material civilization of the Mexico of that day was built. It seems safe to promise that when there is lengthened peace again in Mexico, mining will take its place with the greatest industries of the country—although oil may still retain its present primacy when it, too, can spread out and develop itself.

Mining camps and groups of mining camps dot the country, and whole distinct territories are devoted to the mining, here of silver, there of gold, there of copper, lead, etc. Indeed, the geography of Mexico has had a tremendous effect in the creation there of a country primarily rich in minerals as she is poor in agriculture. Oil is to-day the greatest single wealth of Mexico, but the other minerals have had and will again have their important bearing on her development.

The mineral wealth (oil as well as metals) has as I have noted been the chief attraction which has brought foreign capital to Mexico. The Spaniards and to a lesser extent the Indians before them, mined the mountains of

Mexico, but it remained to foreign enterprise in the time of Diaz to open up the great bonanza sections to scientific development. In the train of this development, came more foreign capital of every sort, for agriculture, for industry, for oil, and for public service investment. This foreign capital, developing Mexico's latent wealth, opened her to the world, and brought forth her great promise of the future, even though it also gave to the revolutionists who overthrew Diaz a handy battle cry of anti-foreignism.

It seems unlikely that without the geographical and geological conditions which offered the wealth of minerals to the development of capital, Mexico would or could have entered upon the modern stage of her development. In that was the hope of the past and in it, too, is the hope of the future regeneration of Mexico. The tempting possibilities of such development are the only bait which will bring back to Mexico the stream of foreign capital to which alone she can look for her prompt salvation, when peace comes at last.

The geography and climate have had their hand, too, in the industrial situation in Mexico. Mining, in the time of Diaz, drained the available labor away from the farms and away from the small factories which then existed. The oil fields have more recently taken a large proportion of the available workers. The supply of labor in Mexico is astonishingly small—the development of the latent labor supplies in the Indian communes waits on peace and education. Temperamentally (and in this we find the hand of climate) the Mexican is not a good factory worker. The raw products which the land produces, sisal hemp, cotton, rubber, etc., all demand for their profitable manufacture large and intricate plants, such as Mexico has not built and for whose operation she has never trained her people. Therefore, save for the cotton factories (which produce only the coarser staples) there is to-day in Mexico almost no industrial development. The lists of industries of which such a manufacturing town as Monterey boasts, include, for instance, candle and match factories employing thirty or forty people, brass bed "factories," where the products of American foundries are put together, soda water factories—the industries which no city in any other land would find worth mentioning. Mexican industry, indeed, waits surely upon the development of the crops of raw materials, upon the education of her laboring classes, and upon the solution of the problems of irrigation and water power.

Geography and climate have been cruel to Mexico,—of this we need not seek to deceive ourselves. But throughout the list of unhappy conditions which has been set down here there runs a promise of advancement and of better things—when peace comes and when foreign enterprise shall again be welcomed. All of the advance which Mexico has made in her long fight against an unkind Nature has been made with the help of foreign energy.

First was Spain, and the 300 years in which she built up the colony to a semblance of a modern state, creating great cities and peace and prosperity. Then, after fifty years of destructive revolution, Diaz, and his wise invitation to and use of foreign enterprises and foreign money. Only in these two periods has Mexico been prosperous.

The greatest advance was under Diaz, when in thirty years Mexico rose from the ashes of her revolutions and flew toward the heights of commercial advancement. In that time her railways were almost all of them built, all the water power which she now has developed, the one great and productive irrigation section—the Laguna cotton district—reclaimed from the desert, the sisal hemp industry created, the factories, such as they are, built and set in operation. Virtually all of these advances were made with foreign capital and under the control of foreign engineers and managers. Success rewarded the faith and the efforts of all who devoted themselves to these developments and it was their conquering of the great natural handicaps of Mexico which made possible the glowing tales of her "treasure-house." When such times as those come again, and only when they come, will the battle against Nature be resumed, and in its resumption, the signs of man's great conquest reappear.

FOOTNOTES

[2] This chapter is based upon the author's article on Mexican Geography contributed to the important *Mexican Year Book for 1920-21*, published in Los Angeles, Calif., concurrently with this volume.

[3] *The People of Mexico*, Book I, Chap. V.

CHAPTER III
THE PEOPLE WHO BUY

A bamboo hut with a clumsy thatch of grass, a hovel of sundried bricks, made, as the Israelites made them, of straw and clay, a shack of unfinished lumber or rotting railway ties topped with a roof of laminated sheet-iron—these are the symbols of the social level of Mexico. Within them all a dirt floor, a box filled with earth for a brazier, two or three earthenware pots, a *metate* over which the woman bends at her endless task of grinding meal for the family cakes of unleavened corn, a few rush mats for beds and a tawdry shrine with a dim light before it—the inert millions of Mexico live to-day as they have lived for a thousand years.

Their minds untutored, their thoughts and desires confined literally to the animal plane, their religious instincts almost entirely superstition, their government the support of rulers upon the vast misery of the lowly, Mexico finds her parallels only in China and in Turkey. And Mexico is at our own back door, the cynosure of our most hopeful tradesmen!

Up until ten years ago, there was an aristocracy in Mexico counting in its make-up many able men, groups of able men, devoted as far as their lights allowed them, to a paternalistic care of the Indians and peons, and to the development of Mexico as a great, modern state. Under Diaz there was also a slow building of a material civilization, looking, in the future, to the filling of the peon stomach and the lifting of the peon mind through education to the light of the white man's world, to a place in the white man's commerce. It has been the common usage, in this past decade since Diaz fell, to excoriate that aristocracy, to blame it for all the evils of the country, to point with bitter scorn at its wealth, at its material monuments of churches and palaces and mines and railways. And yet, although these ten years of revolutions have been devoted most effectively to the elimination of the Mexican upper classes and of their materialism and its monuments, the condition of the lower classes has not been alleviated by one tiny burden, nor has it been lifted by one hair's breadth.

The Mexicans of to-day are worse off than they were in the days of Diaz; they are worse off than in that wild revolutionary period before Diaz; I am not so sure that they are not in worse condition than they were under the Spaniards, for they seem literally to be sliding back to an era of barbarism like only to that misery which was theirs before the Spaniards came.

We lose sight of the essential fact of Mexico, commercially as well as socially, if we lose sight for one moment of the lowest of the Mexican people. They present to us our first and greatest problem, whether we are traders, missionaries, or those who seek to develop Mexico's resources or to sell her our goods.

It is they who must buy our merchandise or aid our work or operate our factories, mines and oil wells. They were, and are, a vast potential market, a great, slow-moving force for us to re-shape by education into an advanced people, civilized, progressive, using the products of the world and pouring their own products back into the stream of commerce. They offer us an immense, a wonderful well of labor, perhaps a greater contributant to the nation's future wealth than anything else in all Mexico. Because of these potentialities and because of our inability to understand why such possibilities do not find their development, it is vital that we look, clear-eyed and sympathetically, on the one great and overwhelming factor in that hopeless inertia—the ignorance of the mass of the Mexicans.

Mexico is a land of innumerable children. A land where there are twice as many children under ten years old as there are in the United States (in proportion to population). And a land where not one child in six has even the chance to go to school, because there are no schools for them.

The depth of Mexico's ignorance, in childhood and in adulthood, in life and in business, literally passes comprehension. The active, curious minds of the Indian youngsters grow quickly into sodden stupidity; the keen and vivid intelligences of the children of the middle and upper classes expend their growing forces in sensuality and plunge themselves and their country into debilitating excesses—because there is no training to give them a life above the animals.

I have seen, in the seats of government in Mexico, men who know less of world history than a boy in an American high school; I have talked with "experts" of government departments who knew less of their special subjects than did I, a layman. I have seen in the presidential chair men who believed, literally, that the shrunken, sick Mexico of to-day was one of the great, advanced countries of the world—because they had no conception of the development of world civilization.

I have seen, in Mexican homes, the slow murder of Mexican babies, because neither I nor any one else could change the round of tradition, unrelieved by training of any sort, which takes an annual toll of child life in Mexico that is perhaps not surpassed even by the toll of the famine in China.

The chain of tradition links Mexico together, and links her, too, to a past which goes back into the furthest reaches of prehistoric legend.

The ways of modern agriculture are those of the early Aztecs, and modern tools, even, are introduced with the greatest difficulty. The round of life is a brief cycle of dull days, unlivened by any thought or knowledge beyond the confines of a village or a township or a few blocks of a city. The schools, such as they are, are patterned after models long abandoned everywhere else in the world, and are stifled by a traditional belief that war and revolution and the erection of imposing buildings are more important to the progress of the country than the education of its youth.

All this has driven Mexico on through the years handicapped with a load of illiteracy that can well be recognized as the most potent factor in the degeneration that marks her every manifestation to-day.

Only figures can tell, even in part, the depths of that ignorance. Back in 1895, the Mexican government reports (which one must always remember speak as favorably as they dare) showed that only 2,000,000 out of a population of 12,500,000 could read and write! This means that 82 per cent of all the people of Mexico were without these rudiments of learning. By 1900 this percentage had been reduced to 80 and in 1910 the Diaz government claimed that it had been reduced to 78, in other words that of the 15,000,000 population of that year, a little over 3,000,000 could read and write, while nearly 12,000,000 remained in the depths of their ignorance. In 1919, the Carranza government issued a report claiming but a slight advance over these figures in the nine years since the fall of Diaz.

It is literally true that not a tenth of all the people in Mexico have what we would call a common school education, and three out of four cannot read a street sign or scrawl their own names. Indeed, one great British mining company reported that of its 595 Mexican employees, including scores of what we would call skilled workmen, only six, or about one per cent could sign a receipt for the money they were paid.

To those of us who look on through foreign eyes, this condition explains much of Mexico's dilemma, and the point is further clarified when we know that the greatest claim ever made for Mexican education showed but 12,000 schools, with 850,000 pupils enrolled—while the population of children of school age was more than 4,000,000! No single issue is greater or more pressing than education. Yet education waits, as everything in Mexico waits, on peace and better times, on food and on health. And these wait—and more than all, from our selfish interest, business and commerce wait—on education! Around and around the problem swings, and each issue is dependent upon another, and that, then, upon the first.

Of all the complicated, interwoven factors of Mexican life and of the tendencies, this very day, of Mexican business and trade none, however, offers so true an understanding as race. The basis of Mexico's ignorance and the basis of her steel-bound traditions is Indianism. For Mexico's 15,000,000 people include 6,000,000 pure-blooded Indians, of some fifty tribal strains, literal aborigines in their life and in their thoughts. There are, as I have noted, 8,000,000 mixed-bloods, three-quarters of whom are virtually Indians in their way of life and in their outlook upon the world. And there are only 1,000,000 of white strain, mostly Spanish, a group which is to-day without voice in the affairs of the country. Two-thirds of Mexico is Indian, and most of the other third a mixture of Indian and white, a mass with the dark Indian sea below it and virtually no light coming to it from above.

To-day there sifts into the Mexican ruling classes—these same mixed-bloods—hardly a ray of culture, hardly a gleam of a truly broader outlook, to lift them and their people out of the dull cavern of their circumscribed life, or to lead them to the better things of modern civilization and commerce. We talk of the heathen of China, of the darkness of ignorance and superstition in Africa, but in Mexico the churches and the foreign industrial concerns seem to me to face a greater need than in any other country in the world.

For Mexico is at our door, and the cultural traditions of Mexico are those of our own world, the white. For 300 years she was a subject state of Spain, and for all the mistakes of the Spaniards and the Roman Catholic Church, the foundation-stones they laid are as the foundation stones of our own life.

The Indian mass was the great problem of Spain; it was the great problem of Diaz; it is the great problem of all those who would lead her to the ways of the world of to-day. For the past ten years it has been forgotten, lost in the struggles of individual men for personal power. But always those individuals have been swallowed up, without their realizing it, in the mire of Indianism, for Indianism, the very epitome of ignorance, lies there always beneath the Mexico that the world sees, waiting to engulf its own masters and to destroy all social and business progress. The Spaniards and Diaz built above these shifting sands, ever conscious of them, providing against them always. Diaz fell because after he built his foundations he did not reach down into the Indian mass to up-raise them. He fell in his old age, forgetting, as old men forget, the dangers which have been with them through all their life. But before he fell he had laid the foundations, building upon those of the Spaniards and erecting new ones of his own, among them foundations of foreign business, of foreign missions, of foreign schools, business and missions and schools which by their own enterprise and perhaps as much by the examples which they set for Mexican business, Catholic churches and native school teachers, were beginning the great uplift of that vast, inert Indian mass.

The brief rule of Madero (1911-1913) was the link between Diaz and the upheaval of radicalism and Indianism which was to begin with Carranza, in 1914. Then commenced the process of casting away, bit by bit, all the slow-built civilization, all the shallow foundations of commercial prosperity, of Diaz. With Carranza began the upsurgence of the Indian, the terrific push upward of the long-hidden forces of destruction which had been held in check, not only for the thirty years of the Diaz peace, but for all the four centuries since the Spaniards had first come to Mexico.

Primarily, this destruction was marked by the wiping out of the fabric of the promising Mexican educational system—for Diaz had made sound beginnings toward raising the Indians out of the depths of their ignorance. His rule was building a foundation for business and for progress by creating an intelligence which would demand and would develop the better things which white civilization had to offer.

Under Carranza the ideal was not of slow uplift by education and the creation of a substantial economic existence which would make life and peace worth striving for. Carranza and those who followed him under the banner of the revolution have thought little of solid progress. Their ideal has been revolution—the political remedy for the economic ills of the land.

So, despite all the sweeping promises of Carranza and his immediate successors, education and the progress of business, of trade and of development have gone into the discard. With the pressure of the needs of the revolutionary "generals" for greater and greater appropriations for their armies (and for the graft which ate up most of such appropriations), with the ever-widening circle of vampires who fattened on government patronage in every other conceivable way, the money available for education as well as for industrial advancement shrank steadily. Where under Diaz the total annual budget of the government was $50,000,000 a year, with a total appropriation for schools, federal and state, probably less than $4,000,000, Carranza had nearer $100,000,000 and spent less than $2,000,000 a year on education. For Carranza, when the demands of his "generals" for their "share" increased, shut off the federal support of the schools of the City of Mexico and its neighboring villages, and also the sums which in other days had gone to help the poorly provided state governments. He threw the school systems on the hands of absolutely bankrupt cities and towns, with the result that in the City of Mexico alone some 120 schools, half the former number, were closed, and 25,000 children, despite crowding into other buildings, were deprived of education. All this is history. And statistics do not show that there has been any recovery since that day.

The Obregon government, on paper, re-established the federal department of education with a cabinet officer at its head, which was abolished by Carranza as an economy measure. There was some more of the endless Mexican discussion of systems of education, but so far as can be found, no increase in appropriations or in plans for better support of the public schools. All those wait, perhaps, as I have said, on the improvement of business conditions, as the final solution of the business problem waits, I believe, upon them.

But they all wait on something else, which I have mentioned above, and that is the improved physical condition of the Mexican people. Comfort, food and health are as important to mental and moral development as the training of the mind by education. The misery of Mexico is so profound, her crashing inertia so deep-rooted and so self-perpetuating, that it sometimes seems that she can never be cured from within herself. Some outside force must break the circle and this I believe is the great opportunity of the American missions, working in conjunction with the great civilizing energies of American business.

Already something has been done, by great American business concerns, and by American trade unions along the northern border and even within Mexico itself, to improve living conditions. But the terrific chasm of the Mexican mass remains utterly unplumbed, and the childhood of Mexico and the manhood and womanhood of Mexico wait, hungry because their food does not feed them; in discomfort because their long traditions do not let them even desire comfort; in sickness because of utter ignorance of the foundations of human health.

Of this last a word must be written here. I have compiled, elsewhere,[4] the astonishing figures bearing upon this question, and have found, in the mass of Mexican official statistics, that the death rate of Mexican babies under one year is nearly twice that of the United States; between birth and ten years, three times that of this country, and that clear through the whole range of Mexican life, from two to four times as many Mexicans die in each thousand as die in the United States at the same ages. The average life of every Mexican born is but 15 years, while in the United States it is about 35 years, and half of the Mexicans born this year will be dead before they are 7 years old, while in the United States half of all the babies born will live to be 42 years old.

High death rate means sickness. Experts estimate that for each death in the United States there are 300 days of severe illness and 6,000 days of indisposition or slight illness, spread over the average 35 years of American life. But in Mexico the average age of death is 15 years, so that the days of sickness must be crowded into less than half the space of time they cover in the United States.

In Mexico, almost no care, as we conceive it, is given to the sick. The government reports show that only one-quarter of all the deaths reported in the country are listed as "classified by the doctor"—in other words, there is no medical attendance at all in three-quarters of all the fatal illnesses in Mexico. It is well known to those who know that unhappy land that in the case of illness, the priest and the doctor are sent for at the same time, the priest to administer extreme unction, the doctor to do what he can with a dying patient.

This factor of ill-health in Mexico is one of the most terrible of all the pictures of her misery, perhaps the most potent element in the national ineptitude. No one who is continually ill can be greatly interested in progress, mental, or moral, or industrial, for illness is the greatest force working against the material advancement of the people and of the country. And upon material advancement, upon the increase of income and the increase of needs physical and cultural (as the money comes to procure them) we must build the solidity of the Mexican people that are to be, as well as the trade which we seek to gain from them.

Out of this picture of darkness, then, comes opportunity and with opportunity the dawning of a new day in Mexico. Because ill health is so great a factor as it is, there is something that we can attack and can conquer. Because education is at the low ebb that it is, there is something which we can do that is direct and tangible, when the means are put into our hands.

There is hope in Mexico, and that hope is tied up with the opportunity for foreign help, which is actually, and even more potentially, the most disinterested and direct force working on conditions in Mexico to-day. The land is so torn by personal politics, so nearly ruined by the exactions of unthinking government, so much the football of well-deserved calumny, that this single ray of clean, clear light can be recognized by all as one of the great hopes in the horizon to-day. That hope must be made to dawn, and it is well for us to consider how that dawn may be assured, and how the day which must follow may be firmly grounded on economic permanence, on social stability and on the comfort, health, education and industrial progress of the Mexican people.

This is the field wherein I believe that the coöperation of the American companies established in Mexico and the American missions operating there will bring about a solution of the ultimate Mexican problem. For the companies, ready and anxious as they appear to be to serve, would, through the missions, find a means wherein their money and the great force of their prestige would have efficient direction. The foreign oil, mining and railway corporations will not hesitate, I believe, to place their resources and their opportunities at the disposal of workers whom they are convinced can truly improve the morale and thus the productive capacity of the workers upon whom their business depends. Heretofore there has been mutual misunderstanding. The companies have not always found the mission workers as efficient as they would like, and the missionaries have been quite ready to suspect the companies of representing "predatory capital" with the ambition, not merely of making their business profitable, but of putting down the "devoted" leaders of the people or of forcing American intervention at once.

I have faith in both the companies and the missionaries, and I believe that in the new political crisis which Mexico is bringing upon herself as this is written (and which she may have tumbling about her ears before it is printed) these two must reach out, and will reach out, to clasp hands and go on together.

Both have done wonderful things for Mexican education, the missions through the conscious development in Mexico of the ideal of education for service, and to the end of raising and training leaders for the Mexican masses, and the companies through isolated examples of truly constructive welfare and educational work.

Probably the most outstanding example of the educational achievements of American corporations was that of the trade schools which were organized and operated by the National Railroad between 1890 and 1912, under the direction of E. N. Brown, president of the National Railways—one of the "pernicious foreigners" who were exiled under Carranza's "nationalization" of the railway properties in 1914. These railway schools trained between 15,000 and 18,000 Mexican mechanics and engineers, taking boys of 14 and 15, paying them first 62 cents a day and gradually increasing that until, after four years' training, they were receiving three and a half pesos a day. They were then ready to take positions as skilled workers in the railway shops or on the locomotives or, if they chose, in other industries. The railway placed no limitation on them, holding that the company benefited in the increase of the efficiency of the Mexican worker wherever he might be.

The whole scheme of this work, including the paying of apprentices while learning, was the broadest kind of educational service, taken up, to be sure, because the railway company needed mechanics and trainmen, but with an effect on Mexico and on the creation of the so-called Mexican "middle class" (the buying and building as well as the elevating element in any population) which is still felt through the chaos of revolutionary destruction.

To-day the greatest industry of Mexico is the production and refining of petroleum, and foreign companies, of course, control it. Much genuinely helpful welfare work is being done by them, including not only schools for children but training schools for workers as well. In addition the very conscious plan of increasing wages until unskilled labor now receives a minimum of $2 a day is having a remarkable effect upon the standard of living and upon the buying capacity (as well as upon the efficiency) of the Mexicans of the Tampico oil section. There is much undigested prosperity, and agitators are creating trouble as far as they can for the foreigners, but on the whole the effect on the material well-being of the peon has been advantageous. It is inevitable that a continuation of this attitude should bring forth a vastly increased civilization at least in this one section of Mexico.

Education has been pushed forward by the companies, and in the model villages such as the town of Terminal (across the river from Tampico on the property of the Doheny companies) really excellent schools are maintained with Mexican teachers under American supervision.

Conditions in the oil country outside the private company towns are, however, deplorable, presenting a contrast which is not without its mighty lesson for us all. The graft and incompetence of the present ruling classes of Mexico have regarded the prosperous oil towns only as the most luxurious of posts for influential favorites. The educational conditions of Tampico, where in a city of more than 100,000 people there are only twenty government primary schools with an attendance of 4,500 pupils, beggars description. Yet the foreign companies have been called on regularly to support the Tampico schools, just as they are called on to pay for pavements, sanitation, etc. And this money has gone, hardly a single dollar into the work for which it was collected, but countless thousands into the bottomless pit of revolutionary graft.

But for all the unfortunate conditions of the moment, the possibilities of the foreign corporations aiding in the uplift of the Mexican mass throughout the country is one of the encouraging phases of the Mexican trade and business problem. It links up definitely with the solution (on which we shall touch, in later chapters) of the parts of the question which deal with other elements than the human equation. The beginning which has been made in Tampico, chiefly by the great American companies, carries with it an import far greater than the mere contrast between their trim little company villages and schools and the ugly squalor of the Mexican towns. Somehow, out of the dark present, American business has learned how closely it is linked with the welfare of the human element in its scheme. They have learned how the simple man, how his happiness and prosperity, are wrapped up with the prosperity and success of every enterprise which remotely touches him.

Until these recent years, and through these American corporations, there has never been scientific welfare work in Mexico, there has never been considerate treatment of the workers, little study of their weaknesses and their needs. If we contemplate that, in its bare truth, we can begin to understand something of the importance of even the relatively little work which has been done of late. Perhaps the greatest potentiality of the future of the human side of the Mexican market lies in the broad extension of that genuinely American attitude toward the masses of the country.

I have advocated the union of the forces of American missionaries and American corporations in Mexico. I believe that this will bring great good and will eventually, as it has done in this country, bring a higher efficiency of labor and a larger market for the things which this country can export to Mexico. The desertion of the masses by the revolutionary government and the exile of the natural aristocracy, have brought the human problem of the country home with tremendous force to the foreigners. It lies to-day almost solely in their hands, and seems likely to wait long for a rescue or aid from any other source whatever.

For the missionaries, education and improved economic conditions amongst the workers is indispensable—they are the tools and the signs of their great plan of regeneration. For business, the encouragement of religion and education which the mission schools give promises that improvement in the laboring population and in the buying capacity of that population which is demanded by the advancement of their business. Somehow that buying population which I have set at 3,000,000 must be increased. Somehow the efficiency of the laboring group (which numbers little more than the buying public) must be increased. Only one way is open—to make the masses better men, happier men, more cultured men. The ignorance of Mexico, the inefficiency which results from that ignorance, the low standard of living which keeps the people from those "wants" which make luxuries into necessities and so improve trade by widening the eddies of demand—all these affect us all in Mexico.

Trade follows education. It follows the missionaries of business and of religion. It thrives alone on the prosperity of peoples. To-day these factors of trade in Mexico are only depressants—in the future they must and surely will be changed slowly into booming creators of trade. But so long as the chief item of import is food and so long as the productive capacity of the Mexicans is only half developed, so long will the market in Mexico swing at its lowest ebb.

FOOTNOTES

[4] *The People of Mexico.* Mexican health is treated directly in the chapter on "Vitality," pp. 86-109, and indirectly in the chapter on "Climate," pp. 131-151.

CHAPTER IV
THE CREDIT OF MEXICO AND OF THE MEXICANS

The Mexican government to-day is bankrupt, and Mexican business is bankrupt. The most sanguine propagandists of the revolutionary governments can offer nothing better than promises to offset the obvious facts of Mexican finance. The government to-day owes nearly a billion dollars—including unpaid interest on her debts for eleven years. Commercial credit has reflected the ghastly vision of government bankruptcy, because the ingrained principle of Mexican politics has been the subservience of economic progress to political exigencies.

The history of Mexican revolutionary government has been marked by the steady suction of business into the maelstrom of political horror. This began in the earliest years of the rule of Carranza (1914-1920). For five years Carranza carried on a deliberate campaign to destroy the banks, as the representatives of the capitalists. He succeeded, despite all the magnificent resiliency of business. He swamped the country with paper currency; he withdrew the metallic reserves of the banks until their bank notes reached almost the degradation of his own issues. He made Mexico into a land of thieves, and gave their thievery the cloak of government sanction—as of one thief underwriting the ventures of another.

When her banks were gone, Mexico had nothing left but her mines and her oil, for Mexico creates virtually no wealth. She manufactures nothing and exports nothing save the ultimately exhaustible resources of her soil. Mining flourished during the war, with allied governments supporting the lead and silver markets, and oil has flowed on and continues to flow, giving Mexico herself only the curse of incalculable unearned wealth for the personal loot of her government officials.

Credit was Mexico's great asset under Diaz—he spent years in establishing it and upon it he built the nation. To-day in Mexico there is no credit. There is gold in circulation and the sight of gold is encouraging to the business man. But the gold in Mexico circulates because there is no credit; no man trusts another and none trusts the promises of the government. Mexico cannot to-day issue paper money, and her heavily alloyed silver coin is on a par with her gold only because an artificial scarcity is maintained in order to increase the value of silver as the change needed in business.

Mexico is one of the great potential markets of the world. The American manufacturer can justly look to it for an outlet for his wares. But a market is useless until the buyer can pay for his goods. Mexico is not yet a place to dispose of what we make until she can pay for what she takes. The credit situation is the crux of Mexico, and the crux of the credit situation is the political chauvinism which, eight years ago, set out deliberately to destroy that credit, because credit was capitalism and capitalism was unfriendly to the self-appointed leaders of the proletariat and, more important still, was said to be the enemy of that world radical movement to which the Mexican revolutionary leaders look so smugly to save them from interference in their orgy of loot and glory.

When Diaz left the presidency in 1911, there were $35,000,000 in the national treasury, and Mexico's credit was such that she could float at par a national bond issue drawing 4½ per cent. To-day the unpaid interest on her public obligations exceeds $150,000,000 and she cannot at any price borrow a cent on any security less than the indorsement of the government of the United States of America.

This is the way the situation is expressed in cold figures. But Mexico is a land of infinite resource, both natural and diplomatic, and nations in worse condition than this have been taken in hand by great bankers and placed upon their financial feet. Any Mexican official can explain Mexico's condition convincingly—the long years of revolution, the paralyzation of industry through destruction and through the prices and want brought to all the world by the Great War. It is therefore of no really deep significance, they say, that Mexico owes millions of dollars, and that she is to-day suing for favor in the world's money markets. But there is a deep and fundamental cause which is back of her financial bankruptcy, back even of its merely economic causes in wrecked mines and abandoned factories, in ranches stripped of millions of head of cattle which bandits have killed for their hides.

The real bankruptcy of Mexico goes deep down into the minds of men, Mexicans and foreigners, government officials and rabid interventionists alike. The bankruptcy of Mexico is a sickness born of broken faith, a moral bankruptcy that is ugly with human greed and hopeless with nervous fear.

The trouble with Mexico to-day is that Mexicans as well as foreigners have ceased to believe in Mexico.

At the time of my several recent visits to Mexico, I did not go as a stranger to the country. I had watched her develop during six years prior to 1910, under the peace and prosperity of the Diaz régime. Understanding something of the native psychology and much of that of the foreigners, I was prepared to find that a good deal of the seriousness of the situation was due to panicky fear and distrust one of another. What I was not prepared for was a condition where every incident, every situation, every tight-strung nerve of potential strength or weakness led down pell-mell paths to a deep ravine of utterly blasted faith not only in present conditions in Mexico, but in the possibility of the country's ever crawling back to her old serenity and strength in any measurable time.

Mexico, as most Americans do not realize, considers herself to have been at peace for the past five years, for the bandits were in the hills and most "revolutionary" outbreaks were being successfully nipped. Yet in the important city of Monterey, typical of the interior of Mexico, the damage done "in the revolution" remains untouched. On the main plaza the stones that are left of the beautiful old Casino, burned by Carranza's soldiers six years ago, have barely been moved from the roadway. Smoke-stained shells of buildings rise here and there, and in the suburbs bullet-ridden windows still remain in fine private houses and factories. The once paved streets are full of unexpected bumps, the roads leading to the smelters and out into the country are cut deep with ruts and puddles and railway crossings are all but impassable, even to skipping Fords. The street cars limp and bump and leak, and the very civic improvements seem installed with a fatalistic certainty that they will soon be destroyed.

There is industry and there is business in Monterey, each of a kind. In the old days there were two great smelters, foreign owned, a steel plant and a brewery, besides three railway shops and miscellaneous other factories. Most of the miscellaneous factories closed long ago, but the smelters and the steel plant kept going in good order—as long as war prices sustained them. Now, one of the smelters has closed, for London has ceased holding up the lead market, and the other (owned by the American Smelting and Refining Company) continues only because it uses the ore from its own mines. During the war the steel plant was handled by the United States War Trade Board, the great organization which harnessed our own industries to war needs, and 80 per cent of its product was, by agreement, sold in the United States and in Cuba—at war prices. When the war ended, the Monterey steel plant was forced to curtail, and to-day the great blast furnace is cold and only a Mexican government order for a few thousand tons of steel rails keeps the rolling mill moving.

The railway shops are content with the most perfunctory of repairs, and are more remarkable for the appalling array of rusted and rotted engines (I have counted 150 engines out of commission in the Monterey yards) and for the wrecks of burned freight cars which fill their sidings than for any activity which inspires their machinery.

The few factories which operate are sustained, in their turn, by the high prices which even the staples of existence command in Mexico. Three small cotton goods factories, reopened five years ago, get prices only a few cents below those paid for imported goods, to whose cost in this country is added a heavy import duty. The brewery keeps running, although it pays the government a tax of 100 per cent on its product—estimated to be $1,000 in American gold per day.

Retail trade goes on, throughout Mexico, but the sales are greatly curtailed and the prices are out of reach of the masses, being twice to five times those of the last normal period, 1912. Stocks are hopelessly depleted, for no merchant will keep a large supply of goods on hand, for fear not alone of the long-promised drop in the world market, but of what will happen in Mexico to-day or to-morrow or next week.

Moreover, all business is on an absolutely cash basis, and for "hard" money—gold and silver—alone, whether the trade be wholesale or retail. In Mexico to-day credit is practically unknown, either amongst Mexicans or between Mexican houses and those with whom they deal abroad. There is a stringency of currency, due to the destruction (for various reasons soon to be noted) of all forms of paper money. Mexico is spending literally her economic life blood, gold and silver, and her great resources are wasting and rotting because there is no money with which to develop them or to move them.

Those are simple conditions, patent to any observer who stays longer than the few hours or a day allowed the busy junketer on his trip through "prosperous Mexico." Back of these conditions, however, are facts which are as incontrovertible and menacing. The closing of the smelters has back of it the conditions of mining, in a country which for centuries has depended on its mines for its existence as an economic entity. Even through the war, with war prices for metals, the mines which were producing were only those with high grade ores, which could bear the risks of banditry, the cost of ponderous freight rates, or could maintain their private railway trains to transport ore which the run-down government rolling stock could not handle. Moreover, even war time prices did not make possible the proper development of the properties, and when the bottom dropped out of the lead and copper markets, many of the richest mines closed, because they had not been able or had not dared do enough normal development to keep ahead of the work on the rich veins.

Back of the hand-to-mouth operation of factories and wholesale and retail stores is the situation with regard to currency and banking. Money in Mexico is worth, at legal interest, 1 per cent per month (12 per cent per year) but if you have money, and will take a chance, you can get 5 per cent a month and even more on as good security as the country affords. So few are the men who believe enough in Mexico to take the chance that there is not enough capital even to satisfy the needs of speculators. And can legitimate business expand or even carry its normal load when the money it ought to borrow, the money it has already invested, is worth so much as that? The only form of business which thrives in Mexico is speculation, and I think I am safe in saying that virtually every sign of business activity which any visitor to Mexico sees to-day is speculative at its source or dependent upon speculation.

This speculation finds its chief manifestation in the marketing of food—the distribution of the necessities of life is in Mexico, as elsewhere, the source of sure profit. But in Mexico, so great is the fear of men of what may happen, that the profits of speculation transcend anything known to our busiest food profiteers. The farmers will not take the chances (which include the uncertainties of costly graft) incident to getting freight cars or pack animals as well as the fear of bandits. This allows the speculators, in quick turnovers, to make as much as 200 per cent on a car of corn in a fortnight, and this condition has lasted for nearly eight years.

Another phase of speculative activity is in the importation of foreign goods. The Mexican customs laws are complicated with elaborate classifications, and at best it is something of a speculation for a merchant to import goods in the days of sudden changes in classifications and boosts of tariffs without notice. In addition, however, many favored henchmen of government officials have been given concessions to import all goods free, privileges which it is said they sell to any one who will take the risk for a fixed charge of one-half of the customs fee that would otherwise have been collected. Now and then these favored persons take a flyer of their own and one of them once sent in a carload of shoes, most of which were dumped in Monterey. Having paid no duty, the shoes were sold at prices which demoralized the local market, for the normal duty on a pair of shoes averages $1.50.

Other things "happen." For instance, a favored group gets a trainload of goods—say foodstuffs—at an entry port. Then the government suddenly announces that, effective at once, the high duties on these foodstuffs are to be removed. The goods of those "in the know" go across duty free, and if other merchants telegraph orders to take advantage of the open port, as like as not they find, when the goods reach the border, that the high duties have been put back as suddenly as they were removed.

Such things as these happened with great frequency in the days of Carranza. Perhaps they are not happening now, for Mexico is on her good behavior. But all this has occurred frequently enough to have shaken the faith of simple men. The fear of what may happen to-morrow—things of this sort or something else—stifles business, for business is a timid spirit, and does not recover its confidence quickly.

I hold no brief against the present governments of Mexico. They have been and still are revolutionary governments. They have a natural faith in their own vital importance to Mexico, and consider that whatever it may have cost the country to get such government is money well spent. But for her own sake and for the sake of those of us who are sincerely interested in knowing what troubles Mexico, it seems that we should realize by this frank analysis the lack of faith which I describe.

The situation which I have just outlined is economic, but back of the economic and basically more important is the financial situation. The cause of the economic bankruptcy is to be found in the new conception of the financial organization of Mexico which the Carranza officials have pronounced, and upon which Mexico has been acting for the past seven years.

Let us look for a moment at the financial side of the foreign investments in Mexico, for recent activities on the part of the government seem to admit that Mexico recognizes that an important factor in the present national bankruptcy is the loss of foreign capital. This damming up of the flow of foreign investments has been the result of two distinct situations. First is the outrages, the wanton destruction of foreign property and foreign lives by bandits and revolutionaries. The other is the enactment and partial enforcement of drastic anti-foreign laws.

One of the strongest pillars of the material prosperity of the Diaz time was foreign investments. The bonanza mines had to become paying low-grade business propositions in order to preserve mining as a national asset. The barren agricultural lands had to be irrigated, with water that fell in mountains hundreds of miles away. More than that, Mexico had to begin to build an industrial machine of railroads and factories which would create new national wealth—the economists of even a generation ago realized that no land, however rich, could prosper from her natural resources alone. These were the axiomatic bases of the economic need of foreign money.

The financial need for foreign capital was yet more pressing. At the beginning of the Diaz rule, the trade balance against Mexico was apparently insurmountable, and although year by year it was cut down through the economic development of the country, each year the trade balance has to be evened up. This was the function of foreign investments, and this was the financial reason for its continued encouragement under Diaz. To the last year of his reign, this inflow of foreign money kept coming evenly, in tens and twenties of millions annually. As it came in, balancing the outgo of interest on the national debt and on private loans, it became itself a producer of Mexican wealth, so that in time it would have eliminated the necessity of further forced-draft encouragement for outside investment.

That time had not come in 1911, however, when Diaz left Mexico. But the net result of the stoppage of foreign investment in the revolutionary period which followed is to be found to-day in that unpaid interest of nearly $200,000,000 on government securities alone.

This is no apology for the mistakes of the Diaz régime. The great men of that day built a vast commercial enterprise, the Business of Being the Republic of Mexico, but like many commercial enterprises of the period before the Great War, it had left out the human equation. It was this failure which wrecked the Diaz government in the end, and made such purely paternalistic régimes virtually impossible in Mexico again.

To-day the rulers of Mexico, awake at last to the need for the foreign money which their revolutionary predecessors shut out so stubbornly under the "Mexico for the Mexicans" policy and the socialistic constitution, have been carrying on an active campaign of publicity and official conciliation. The junkets of Chambers of Commerce from all over the United States are part of the big plan. Yet in the hearts of the people, of this country and of Europe, who hold the purse strings, be they bankers or enthusiastic investors of little capital, there lingers and will linger many doubts. It seems likely to be a long day before the foreign investor finds any new faith in Mexico.

But what of Mexico herself? Where lie the financial roots of her lost faith in Mexico's own future? After the economic conditions noted above, they lie in the Mexican currency situation.

To-day Mexico has no currency but gold, silver, nickel and copper coins. There are no bank bills, there is no bankable paper, there are no promissory notes, no checks, no credit. Seven years ago there was no metallic currency whatever, only banknotes, depreciated till a peso (normally worth fifty cents) would hardly pay carfare. During that time the banking business was all but wiped out, and bankable paper disappeared.

Yet back of that period, in turn, was the time of Diaz, when paper money was as good as gold, and the ordinary processes of exchange went on as in any civilized country. Diaz had found, when he came to power, a condition similar to that which exists to-day, with only metallic currency in circulation. He brought in a new financial régime, establishing sound banks, which under government control issued paper money. In 1910, the circulating medium of the country was $150,000,000, of which $65,000,000 was banknotes, accepted on an absolute parity with the $85,000,000 of gold and silver. This money was, as noted, supplemented by active bankable paper circulating freely in business. To-day, by contrast, the government admits that there is less than $50,000,000 (I personally think it is very much less) of gold and silver money in the country—to transact the business (on a cash basis) of nearly 15,000,000 people!

The loss of $100,000,000 of the circulating medium of the country (to make no estimate of the loss and inconvenience due to the destruction of credit) is the work of the revolutions of the past eleven years.

It was Carranza who started the paper money orgy. In the course of three years he issued probably 2,000,000,000 pesos of paper currency—the exact records, if kept, have never been made public. Through this means he destroyed the confidence of the public in paper money, and ultimately, when he came to full power, wiped out of existence the whole system of Banks of Issue established by Diaz.

The first of the Carranza paper money was issued in Chihuahua, and was accepted at its face value. Diaz had taught the people, down to the humblest peon, to accept paper money, and the bayonets of the Carranza troops convinced any who doubted the quality of the new issue. It was a good scheme for financing a revolution—till Villa drove Carranza out of Chihuahua and declared Carranza money worthless and its possession a political crime. Now Villa money was issued, and was forced upon the people at the points of new bayonets, and as the various chieftains chased each other over the country the money of the towns fluctuated with the identity of the conqueror. Metallic currency disappeared completely and the value of paper money fell by jolts to a few centavos on the peso.

These were the days when men who were paid in American money lived like kings. House rent was fifty cents a month; light, gas and water cost a dime. You could travel hundreds of miles in a Pullman for a dollar, and settle all your old debts for two per cent of the original figure. Food prices went up, of course, and the natives, mostly paid in the depreciated paper, suffered terribly. Starvation followed in waves, and the mortality in the cities was appalling.

The value of paper money fluctuated over night, and after closing hours each day, there was a scampering of merchants to sell the currency taken in during the day. They bought New York drafts, worn American bills, diamonds, carriages and real estate, at prices whose rise could not possibly keep up with the fall in the value of paper money.

Early in the excitement Carranza had begun to repudiate his various issues of currency. The reason given was a real one—that they were being counterfeited everywhere, a process simple enough, for the original issues were themselves crudely printed on ordinary paper. At first the Carrancistas had attempted to keep up with the avalanche of counterfeits by requiring that all paper money on hand in banks, stores and private tills be submitted regularly for inspection. Not even the government "experts" could tell the bad from the good, however, and they ended by declaring all of the money submitted by their political friends to be all right, and confiscating, as counterfeit, a large and fixed percentage of that owned by men of doubtful "loyalty." The process did not tend to increase the public confidence in the administration.

The final issues of Carranza revolutionary paper money came from Vera Cruz in 1915. This money alone was recognized as a part of the Carranza government obligation, and $8,000,000 was set aside in the Carranza financial plans for its redemption. This last paper money, issued after Carranza was recognized by the United States, consisted of engraved notes, known as "infalsificables" or "uncounterfeitables." These were issued at 10 centavos on the peso, and the government was pledged to "redeem" them. This is being done, but not by anything so simple as paying honest money for them (which would put them, perhaps, into general circulation). Instead, all who pay direct taxes are required to return a surtax of the face value of their taxes in these "infalsificables." A friend of Carranza wrote that "this was a beautifully simple and ingenious scheme." It is that still, for those favored ones who control the remaining supply of the notes and sell them at advanced prices to the taxpayers who have to have them—mostly the big foreign mining and oil companies.

The story of the paper money days in Mexico, and the fact that of the billions issued but $8,000,000 is recognized as a just debt, may stir the indignation, and it certainly clarifies our understanding of Mexico's lost faith in her rulers. But in point of actual fact, the destruction of the banking and credit system of the country, which was a corollary of the paper money orgy, was far more terrible and cast an even more lasting blight on the standing of the government.

Early in his revolutionary career Carranza was at odds with the banks. He considered it an unfriendly act, one "taking advantage of the unlettered," for the banks to use their knowledge of financial conditions to profit from the fluctuations of his paper currency. He also found the banks "reactionary" in their refusal to use their standing to assist him in making his money popular, and he charged openly that the banks had "combined to discredit the government." On his entry into Mexico City he endeavored to coerce banking officials personally, and jail was sometimes the boarding place of bank managers and bank presidents, when they refused to unlock the vaults to government "inspection."

The wrecking of the banking system extended over more than a year. Huerta, who preceded Carranza in the presidency, took the first forced loans of $5,000,000 from the banks, allowing them to issue new paper currency to cover this coin taken out. Carranza, on gaining control of Mexico City, found the forced loan idea convenient, for he was in sore financial straits.

As one chronicler has it, "Money had to be found.... The money in the banks was the only money available, and it was taken as the only way out of a very difficult situation."[5] In its statement of debts, however, the Carranza government recognized these forced loans to a total of $20,000,000, none of which has been paid in six years.

The Carranza "loans" from the banks inevitably shook their credit and with it the credit of every business man and business organization, and inevitably the credit of the Mexican government itself. Banknotes dropped in value and although they never reached the low mark touched by government paper, their fall to 75, to 50 and finally 30 per cent of their face value reduced in like manner the value of all bank deposits, and finally brought banking transactions to a stand-still. The process of final destruction of the banks began with the edict of September 26, 1915, abolishing out of hand the Huerta concession which had allowed some of the banks to issue additional paper currency to cover the Huerta "loans." The banks were required to bring their reserves up to the old basis in forty-five days, and despite the blow to their credit, this was accomplished. On November 10, however, another Carranza edict reduced the recognized bank reserves by requiring that silver coins be estimated at their bullion, instead of their face value. This storm was weathered, in its turn, and nothing further was done for nearly a year, although during that time the breach between Carranza and the banks was continually widening.

An edict of September 15, 1916, required that the banks should have in their vaults within sixty days enough gold and silver to redeem at par every banknote which they had in circulation, currency which had been issued under concessions allowing a banknote circulation twice the total of the bank reserves in metal and bankable paper. The decree also prohibited the banks from doing business with the public until the conditions set down were fulfilled. In other words, liquidation of notes and deposits was stopped, and the life blood of banking, the active turning over of funds in the course of business, was cut off. Finally, on December 14, 1916, the *coup de grace* was given, and the banks were officially closed to all business excepting the collection of bills receivable in the depreciated currency of the banks themselves.

Thus by a series of cumulative blows the whole Mexican national banking system which had been built up under Diaz was destroyed utterly. At the time the final blow was given, banknotes were accepted at about 30 per cent of their face value, and had apparently reached stability. Bankers assure me that had they been allowed to operate, even under the conditions then prevailing, they could eventually have pulled themselves and much of the business of the country out of the hole. It is also interesting to remember that the franchises of the Banks of Issue were to expire in 1922, time sufficient, under careful government leadership, for them to wind up their affairs and furnish a solid financial basis for the erection of some new form of national currency.

The Mexican governments, one after the other, have lent what prestige they had to a proposed and elaborate new banking law, based on a "Sole Bank of Issue." From Carranza's time the men in charge of the government finances apparently believed that this system could be established on the wrecks of the ruined Banks of Issue. Up to the present this has not yet been attempted, for Mexico was and is in no mood to receive any form of paper currency or government banking, however it may be guaranteed.

It was inevitable, after the banks were closed, that the country should go back to a metallic basis. This was made more difficult, however, by the government's decree, recently reiterated in the summer of 1921, making illegal the circulation of American silver and banknotes. This plan, although it brought out the Mexican gold and silver which had been hoarded, inevitably cut down the circulating medium of the country to absolutely inadequate proportions, even though American money could easily have been obtained to provide enough currency to tide over the crisis.

There were many difficulties connected with the establishment of gold and silver again, but most of them had to do with the scarcity of these mediums. There was a further complication for which no one was responsible. This was the phenomenal rise in the price of silver during the Great War. This early became a crisis, for first the silver pesos became more valuable as bullion than the fifty cents (American money) at which they had been fixed in the time of Diaz, and soon even the subsidiary coins, of a lower silver content, became worth more than their legal value in gold. The export of silver coins had to be stopped by government order, and under the guidance of American monetary experts the recoinage of silver in smaller pieces was begun. To-day this money is in general circulation, accepted at face value for the simple and deliberately created reason that it is issued only as the crying demands of business for change force it out. The new pesos are about half the bullion value of the old, and the subsidiary coins are even less valuable in proportion.

Needless to say, this change in the size of the silver coins had an unfavorable effect on the public mind, already on edge over the various financial coups of the Carranza government. This was aggravated by a destructive form of favoritism by which a few men were allowed, under Carranza, to buy up and export the old silver coins, a form of graft which amazes and disgusts the observer and also, be it noted, made the money shortage greater and less easy to endure.

The ruin of the economic structure of Mexico lies bare for any one to see, and beneath it is the rotted structure of the old financial system. The closing of the banks, the destruction of credit, the shutting off of the relief which might have been given by the use of American currency, seem at the root of most of the ills which then beset Mexico, because they are at the root of the lack of faith of the people and their fear of the caprices of the morrow. For instance, to-day in Monterey, the great industrial center of northern Mexico, there are no banks save two private houses where money can be left on deposit, and a few exchange offices. Where, in 1910, the four Banks of Issue had more than $10,000,000 out in industrial, mining and farm loans, there is hardly as much as $250,000 loaned to-day, and that is by American banks on the border. The safe commercial paper which circulates in Northern Mexico is checks on American banks. The drafts of strong mining and oil companies form the chief basis of money transfer, and are shipped from place to place all over Mexico. Optimists call this a peaceful penetration of American credit into Mexico, and so it is, but all that can be done from outside of Mexico is but a drop in the bucket compared with her financial needs. Credit within and without must be established, and that is a problem which rests with Mexico alone.

To understand at all the mountain of distrust which looms before her, it is necessary to set down, briefly, the condition of the Mexican foreign debt.

The external government debt is $173,000,000, and on this interest has been defaulted for more than eight years, a total of $50,000,000 remaining unpaid. The internal national debt is $67,000,000 and the defaulted interest $20,000,000. State and other debts (save railroads), which have been guaranteed by the government are $33,000,000 and $10,000,000 in interest.

The bonds of the National Railways of Mexico, guaranteed by the Mexican government, total $239,000,000, the interest defaulted being about $75,000,000.

With other items, and counting alone the debts guaranteed by the credit of the government, these obligations total $603,000,000, and the unpaid interest thereon is over $155,000,000. Unguaranteed state and city bond issues, the $20,000,000 recognized as due the banks for "loans," and $8,000,000 with which to redeem outstanding fiat currency bring the total up to a principal of $779,120,915. Nearly eight hundred million dollars, and defaulted interest to nearly two hundred million!

From time to time, and government after government, treasury officials have come to New York to arrange for the refunding of this debt. The plan is usually for New York bankers to loan Mexico $300,000,000, refund the whole debt, eliminating some items (notably by a reduction of the bond issue of the railroads) and take as security the Mexican government's pledge of a portion of the customs duties.

The answer to this proposition has been astonishingly to the point. No Mexican guarantee of customs receipts has interested the bankers unless it was backed by the United States government, presumably with a collection agency of American marines, as in Haiti and Honduras to-day. The most interesting development in answer to the Mexican suggestions of refunding was the appointment of one of the most impressive international banking committees ever created some three years ago. This was headed by J. Pierpont Morgan and announced that its purpose was "the protecting of the holders of securities of the Mexican republic and of the various railway systems of Mexico and generally of such other enterprises as have their field of action in Mexico." It would seem that the probity of the Mexican government, both as to its debts and as to its willingness to repay the losses of foreign investors was slightly under suspicion in the financial circles of the world, a suspicion which is shared by no other Latin-American country save those in actual and admitted bankruptcy.

FOOTNOTES

[5] E. D. Trowbridge. *Mexico Today and Tomorrow*, p. 198.

CHAPTER V
OUR BILL AGAINST REVOLUTIONARY MEXICO

The American after-dinner orator roars his boast of "two billions of American dollars in Mexico" and moans his claim of "a billion of damage" done to those pioneer American dollars. Whereupon the Mexican (of whatever political complexion) wails protest that three-quarters of those American dollars were made out of Mexico herself, and our State Department, which alone might clarify the matter, perforce keeps silence. Up to the present time few have attempted to bridge the gulf between the orator and the Mexican and no one that gulf between the orator and the State Department. We live in an age of "convictions" and we choose our figures according to our beliefs.

Fifteen years ago an American consul in Chihuahua, Marion Letcher, wrote a report in which he estimated (frankly without figures) that the total foreign investments in Mexico were $1,641,054,180, distributed as follows:

American	$1,057,770,000
British	321,302,800
French	143,446,000
Various	118,535,380
Total	$1,641,054,180

These figures have been assailed, especially as regards the comparatively small sum alloted to the British, but they remain to this day the only official estimate available. I have, however, been able to find another compilation, worked out also by Americans, but this by the research departments of several large banking groups, with full access to all Mexican government figures and to the stock books of most of the great American companies. The total, which is for 1914, before the vast bulk of the investment in oil, is almost identical, but the distribution is startlingly different:

American	$655,000,000
British	670,000,000
French	285,000,000
German	75,000,000
Spanish, Dutch, etc.	190,000,000
Total	$1,875,000,000

These figures claim to include the foreign investment in the National Debt of Mexico and are said to estimate the actual distribution, as far as can be worked out, of the holdings of the securities of all companies operating in Mexico. Consul Letcher's figures were conceivably based largely on the nationality of the corporations alone. On the other hand, Europe contributed more than half the invested capital of such important groups as the National Railways of Mexico, made up of companies which were all incorporated under American laws.

When this new compilation of investment distribution first came to my hands, I was, I may admit, inclined to "split the difference." As careful a study of the American investment field as it is possible to make has, however, convinced me that the new figures are much more nearly correct than those of Consul Letcher with one exception. I do not believe that they include all the American investment in the Mexican government, state and municipal bonds held abroad.

On the other hand, neither Consul Letcher's figures nor the other compilation represent the actual full value of American investments in Mexico at the fall of Diaz in 1911. It is important that this fact be remembered because by that date the moneys which had gone into Mexico for foreign enterprise had increased many fold through the energy which went with them and pushed them forward to success. I believe that the original American investment had grown, by 1911, to fully $2,000,000,000, but in order to be absolutely just from the Mexican viewpoint we can discuss the damages on the basis of the actual cash invested—the loss, incidentally, looms even greater. On the other hand, we must not forget that however the Mexicans may claim that the increase in values represents an "exploitation" of their country's resources, the concomitant advance in all values throughout the land in the era of Diaz was almost entirely the direct result of those same foreign enterprises.

From many sources, including of course the two authorities which have been quoted, I have estimated the American investment of actual cash capital and have set against it the losses in actual physical damage and in ruined business, since 1910, as follows:

American Capital in Mexico

	Original Investment	Physical Damage	Actual Losses
Railroads	$150,000,000	$30,000,000	$60,000,000
Oil	200,000,000	5,000,000	100,000,000
Mines	200,000,000	15,000,000	100,000,000
Lands and cattle	50,000,000	10,000,000	20,000,000
Industries and public service	50,000,000	10,000,000	20,000,000
Total	$650,000,000	$70,000,000	$300,000,000

Damage claims aggregating $500,000,000 are said to have been filed with the American State Department, but no official confirmation of this has ever been forthcoming. However, the claims which Americans have against Mexico, whether filed in the State Department or not, must be divided into two categories, the actual and the potential damage, and perforce includes also the claims due for loss of life and personal damages.

The actual harm already done includes: physical damage to property; unwarranted and illegitimate taxes which approach confiscation; destruction of property values through such taxation and through the prevalence of banditry; destruction of property values by the driving out of stable government; destruction of the financial and credit system of the country through government decrees and repudiations; losses in legitimate profits which would have been made during the recent eras of high prices; actual loss in market value of property through the estrangement of the foreign capital which alone, in Mexico, presents a reliable buying element; destruction of property values through the exile of the foreigners who formed the industrious and capable organization which maintained those values.

The potential damages are chiefly those which come from the fact that there hangs over all foreign property in Mexico to-day, and has hung for five years, a sword of Damocles in the threatened confiscation of such property under the radical "nationalization" plans of the revolutionary governments. These, briefly, provide that: foreign corporations and individuals are incompetent to own property in Mexico unless they renounce their citizenship and appear only as Mexicans before the Mexican law; the government may appropriate all large tracts of land, giving in return unguaranteed state agrarian bonds of virtually no value;

the government may "nationalize" the oil in the ground, making it subject to the denouncement of any one, whether the property owner or not, when the whole oil-producing organization of Mexico to-day is founded on the principle of the oil belonging to the land itself; no foreigners, under any conditions, may own any land within sixty miles of the frontier or thirty miles of the seacoast.

Lastly, and in a group by itself, are the damage claims arising from the killing of nearly 600 American citizens in Mexico since the Madero revolution began in 1910. The claims for these outrages and for the maiming and raping of many hundreds more occupy a class by themselves, and will, we may confidently believe, be the first which will be paid when Mexico returns to the ways of civilization.

Just here we can imagine the official Mexican "press department" preparing to state that "Mexico has always paid her bills, including all damage claims." This, however, is not quite literally true. She has paid foreign damage claims at the muzzles of foreign cannon, to be sure, and President Diaz, in that long rule which many call "the anomaly of Mexican history" paid all the bills presented to him. But the only "convention" which ever sat to adjudicate American damage claims was hardly the success that would justify any such sweeping assertion of Mexico's probity. In 1840, after years of turmoil, and after a show of force, President Jackson called a convention of Americans and Mexicans together to consider American damage claims. They sat from 1840 to 1842, allowed $2,000,000 in damage claims, rejected $1,000,000 and when they adjourned left $3,000,000 still to be considered. Under an arrangement of twenty installments, Mexico paid three and defaulted the rest. The cash was paid by the United States, and the slate was wiped clean after the Mexican war of 1847-48. Finally, this war, which as schoolboys we were taught to regard as a sort of "blot on the national escutcheon" was the result of continued outrages to Americans and continued diplomatic jockeyings with an Uncle Sam who even then was much the same model of patience which he is to-day.

In the public discussion of the damage which has been done to American properties in Mexico, there has been much emphasis on the potential harm from the so-called "socialistic" or "bolsheviki" tenets of the new Mexican constitution. There have been vast, crippling losses, yet it seems as if most of what we have heard has been the things which will happen if Mexico is allowed to proceed along her present road. There is reason enough for this fear and for this emphasis, and one of the great battles being fought in the world to-day is that which these Americans are putting up not alone for themselves but for the very principles of property rights. But so far Mexico and particularly the wily gentlemen who have occupied the Mexican presidential chair have always tried to get all they could and have often carried the mis-named "American" bluff to astonishing lengths—but have almost as often retired when the game turned against them. They have used the potential damage as a means of extracting an increasing toll of taxes and of loot, and for little else, as yet.

In this chapter I am, as already mentioned, intentionally avoiding taking these "potential damages" into consideration. I feel that we must have, as a starting point, a comprehensible picture of what has already actually happened to American investments in Mexico.

Most of the American money in Mexico went to that country during the thirty-four years of Diaz rule. This period was marked not by blind adoration of the foreigner, as the revolutionists now state, but by a sane and far-seeing realization that foreign capital must come to Mexico if her national and economic potentialities were to be developed. Foreigners were encouraged generously by laws recognizing the privileges of pioneers in protection and in assistance in the form of exemption from taxes during their development period (the term was usually for ten years). The idea was to allow them to import machinery without duties and get on their feet as quickly as possible. Practically none of these companies was given land, for there is no vacant Mexican government land worth having.

The first and the greatest American corporations to enter Mexico were the railroads. These held concessions, made according to law, but Mexico had profited by the American government's experience with its trans-continental lines, and the subsidies and grants were small indeed compared with those given to our Union Pacific, for instance. It is worth noting also that there have never been such scandals as our great railroads reveled in, and that virtually every cent was invested in the lines themselves. The Mexican railway companies which were consolidated in 1907 into the National Railways of Mexico were never paying ventures for the builders, and until the merger few dividends had ever been paid by any of the lines. For about four years following the merger conditions improved greatly, but in 1912 troubles began, and by 1913 all was chaos and destruction.

From then on to to-day, the story of the railways of Mexico has been a tragic romance. It can be reduced to figures, necessarily cold in the telling, but every figure the result of dramatic and crushingly realistic incident. The National Railways of Mexico, a property worth over $250,000,000 as a physical plant alone, was taken over by the Carranza government on December 4, 1914, and since that time the bondholders have received no cent of interest and the physical property has been crushed and battered and all but destroyed. On January 1 of 1921 over $75,000,000 of back interest was unpaid and the defaulted payments on fixed charges is still piling up at the rate of $1,000,000 a month, while the Mexican government is collecting from the operating commission $1,500,000 a month—a sum set by Carranza for the commission to turn in by any means available, as higher rates, scrimping on repairs, deterioration in upkeep.

The confiscation of the railway properties by the Mexican government under Carranza is one of the most astonishing and illuminating pages in the whole story of Carranza's campaign against capital and the foreigners. But although it began with him, it apparently has continued into the rule of his successors—for they seem a part of the revolution of which he was and still is the dominating, sinister genius. Under the terms of the merger of 1907, the Mexican government was given the voting power—but not the title to—50 per cent of the stock of the company, under certain definite conditions laid down by the bondholders. This 50 per cent interest represented no capital invested, nor was it a recognition of any debt which the railways might have imagined they owed the government. It was given outright in consideration of one thing, the guaranteeing by the Mexican government of a return of 4 per cent interest on the bonds of the merged lines. To the merger the government contributed nothing of tangible value—save one short line of railway worth about $5,000. Its permission was needed, perhaps, for the transfer of the railway concessions to the merger, but this would probably have been given without question had it been asked alone. The interests back of the merger believed that the Mexican government guarantee of the interest on the bonds was worth the gift of the voting right of half the common stock—and on this understanding alone it was given.

The taking over of the physical property by the Mexican government followed the American occupation of Vera Cruz in 1914, and shortly afterwards Carranza made his claim official, on the ground of the 50 per cent voting right! On the basis of this right alone the Mexican government to-day holds control of the National Railways of Mexico, a right once given on the solemn guarantee of the interest on the bonds—which has not been paid for eight years—and with the recognized provision that the bondholders should name the president of the lines, and various officials and members of the board—and to-day there is not one official who is not a creature of the government which happens to be in power in Mexico!

Upon such a basis rests the title of the Mexican government to the National Railways. The subsidies paid by the Diaz government in years gone by for construction were given as the subsidies were given to the American railways which crossed the prairies to the Pacific coast—to make such construction possible in recognition of their benefit to the country. The Mexican subsidies were less than those given to the Union Pacific by the United States government and not one touch of scandal (such as marked our own railway development) was ever breathed against that of Mexico. The subsidies give no tangible claim to the lines—and as far as I know have never been advanced as a claim. The only hold of Mexico over those properties is the shadowy title conveyed by the voting right of a block of stock given voluntarily by the bondholders in return for guarantees which have been thrown to the winds for these eight years.

In the period since the government has had control of the lines, the physical property has deteriorated to a point where only the magnificently solid work done by the American builders to-day holds them together. Operated by the Mexicans, with former firemen as general superintendents and minor native clerks as high officials, the properties went their way of slow destruction in the days of Carranza. Since that time, the turnover of railway officials has eliminated many of the employees who were trained under the American executives of the Diaz and Madero time, and to-day the roads are in the hands of men who learned all they know of the railway business from those who in their turn had gleaned their little knowledge from their American chiefs—now gone from Mexico eight years. The result is a ruin comparable to nothing, probably, but the ruin of railway properties in Russia to-day.

Of the more than 800 locomotives owned in 1914, only 333 (by the notoriously inaccurate Mexican government figures) are said to be running. The rest lie at the bottoms of cañons or are rusting in banks of hundreds in shop yards, as I have this year seen and counted over 100 in the one yard of Monterey. The freight cars have decreased from 18,000 to 7,000, and usable passenger cars are virtually unknown off the main lines to-day—all were wantonly destroyed in the early revolution or stolen and converted into dwelling-places for "deserving revolutionaries." Three-quarters of all the bridges on the 8,000 miles of line are damaged, dozens of them beyond repair, thanks to the diabolical perfection of the methods of destruction used by various Mexican patriots. The tie replacements are seven years behind; nearly 20,000,000 are needed, worth over $17,000,000. Other items in the $80,000,000 replacement bill are $30,000,000 for cars, $12,000,000 for locomotives and $4,000,000 for rails.

This loss has been the result of two forms of destruction—the depredations of the fighting factions and the cumulative destruction of neglect and failure in upkeep. Instances multiply. During one month (March, 1914) seventy trains were blown up while running at 30 to 40 miles an hour; the patriots used to connect up their dynamite with electric batteries and then sight along two sticks from their safe retreat in the bushes and so set off the charge under whatever section of the train caught their fancy. At one time in Monterey in 1915, revolutionary troops burned 800 loaded freight cars; their skeletons line the Monterey sidings for all the world to see, to-day. One of the long bridges on the road to Eagle Pass, on the American border, was wrecked by running a train of loaded coke cars with two locomotives on each end out on the bridge, firing the train and blowing up the bridge when the burning coke had heated the steel. A similar trick on the Tampico line was to take out a rail, then set fire to a train of oil cars and run it full speed on the bridge, where it was derailed and the same process was followed as with the coke train.

The rotting of the ties on the road has left most of the branch lines all but impassable, save to the Mexican enginemen who know each bump and are quite willing to "take another chance." The wrecked bridges, jacked up on timbers, have uncomfortable and terrifying "dips." The list can be multiplied indefinitely. Yet perhaps the most expressive sight to be seen in Mexico to-day is those banks of rusting engines, 100 in Monterey, 100 at Aguascalientes, others at San Luis Potosi, Mexico City and Guadalajara. These engines were only slightly damaged when they were side-tracked, but through the failure of the government to furnish repair materials, they have been gradually stripped of parts to repair other engines, the brasses have been carried off and sold for junk and the whole field of ruin left like a desert waste.

There is in the Mexican railway law a provision for compensation in case the railways are taken over "for military purposes." It is estimated that under this law the damages collectable are only $10,000,000 a year—less by $2,000,000 than the default in the fixed charges alone. The estimated $80,000,000 of physical damage (a mere estimate until an actual valuation can be made) is presumably collectable. The bill of the railroads is, however, as follows: Physical losses, $80,000,000; defaulted interest to June, 1921, $75,000,000; total, $155,000,000. It is believed that about one-third of the bonds are held by Americans, so that their loss is over $50,000,000. In addition, there has been an individual loss in the disposal of the bonds by small holders, at sacrifices as great as 80 per cent. It is even said that the Carranza government had hopes of being able to buy up the railway bond issue when its administrative policies had reduced the quotations to less than 30 per cent of par. Only the lack of money prevented this coup for real government ownership, it is said.

In the above, I have treated only with the National Railways of Mexico. Outside of this system the only important lines in Mexico are the Mexican Railway (British owned) which has now been returned to the stockholders but without compensation for damages and the Southern Pacific in Mexico (American owned). The former suffered severe physical destructions, but the latter's bill for damages, while heavy, sinks into relative insignificance.

In the confines of a general study, space can not be given to the sidelights on the Mexican railway situation—a situation almost Teutonic in its colossal blunders, splendidly American in the elements which have gone to save it from utter wreck. The long years of patient railway building, the hundreds of miles of rock-ballasted lines across unproductive wastes, all done under American management, gave Mexico a system which has held together despite the wreckage of bandits and the ravages of time and neglect. The traffic of the nation moves to-day, not in the wheezy trains which the Mexicans maintain, but overwhelmingly in a system of privately owned locomotives and cars operated by the American mining and trading companies at staggering expense. Their 100 locomotives, in perfect repair (kept so in their own shops) and their nearly 3,000 freight cars probably represent half of the railway equipment running on the National Railways to-day, and they probably carry far more than half the freight. They pay full freight rates in addition to furnishing the trains, and although much of this equipment has been taken over by the government as this is written, it is no exaggeration to say that but for these American companies and their magnificent efforts to save what is to be saved of their Mexican properties Mexico would to-day be stagnant,—a land of chaos comparable only to the period of fifty years ago, before Diaz ruled.

The great oil business of Mexico owes its existence primarily to American enterprise. Of the $300,000,000 of cash invested in the oil fields, $200,000,000 is American. To-day, even after the colossal production during the war, only a small portion of this investment has been recovered, for only two purely Mexican companies, the Mexican Petroleum (American) and the Eagle (British) are paying dividends. The oil business in all lands is so speculative that its returns are quoted not as "dividends" or "interest," but as "recovery," for until the great investment in drilling, tanks, pipe lines, refineries and ships is got back, there is no surety that the venture itself will prove profitable. For this reason the losses of the oil companies through the Mexican revolutions can be only an estimate. From sources which I have been able to reach, I place the actual physical losses at about $5,000,000 for the American companies. This seems like a very small item, but it does not count the failures of most of the 300 companies which have put money into Mexican oil or the vast sums paid in taxes or lost through oppression. Nor does it take into consideration the potential losses if Mexico enforces her "nationalization" plan. These last would be legitimately included here, for as I say, they jeopardize the "recovery" of the investment still remaining unpaid for, and Mexican oil stock quotations have suffered as a result. Mexico still threatens to enforce the provisions of the new constitution which make oil the property of the nation and its exploitation a matter of concession, like gold and silver. The oil companies are fighting this plan, for they entered Mexico and invested millions in oil lands and leases from individuals (no land was ever given them) under a mining law which left coal and oil the property of the owner of the land, unlike gold and all other minerals.

The actual bill of our oil companies includes, as the chief single item, a $2,000,000 loss due to the Battle of Ebano, fought over American property in the spring of 1915. Oil, tanks, pipe lines and refinery buildings were destroyed, a single cannon ball igniting a tank containing 850,000 barrels of oil, all of which was burned. The item of direct thievery (largely by federal troops) is only about $300,000, but petty destruction, murderous assaults, the killing of a score of valuable employees and the tribute to bandits and federal "generals" pile the total up. Tribute has been levied, first by the federal Carrancistas, and from January, 1915, to March, 1920, by Manuel Pelaez, the former rebel leader, to a total of about $2,000,000, Pelaez's figure being a regular $30,000 a month up to his joining the successful Obregon revolution in 1920 and so becoming a "federal."

The ravaging of the oil wells is full of picturesque and terrible incident, like the railways. The most striking and costly was the outrage perpetuated by General Candido Aguilar, son-in-law of Carranza. On December 13, 1913, Aguilar demanded, from the Eagle Oil Company (British) tribute to the sum of $10,000. This was not forthcoming so Aguilar proceeded to carry out his threat of "shutting in" the great "El Portrero" well, one of the most famous in Mexican oil history, which had been a steady producer, for two and a half years, of 30,000 barrels per day. He succeeded in capping it, and before the casing was finally blown out, the oil had broken through the ground in dozens of places, including the bed of a neighboring river. The whole countryside was in imminent danger of a terrible holocaust if the oil on the river flowed away and ignited, as it surely would, but by superhuman efforts this danger was averted. But all other attempts to save the oil and repair the damage were almost fruitless, and for months the seepage went on, until at last the well was reduced to salt water and $20,000,000 worth of oil had been lost. This loss is technically British, although it is probable that the bill for damages will fall upon the United States, for it was undoubtedly through the instrumentality of our State Department and its emphasis of the Monroe Doctrine that Great Britain was restrained from taking action.

Another item to be noted is the great Carranza tax system which continued in full force into the era of Obregon and costs the oil companies some $4,000,000 per month. Part of this may be recognized in time as legitimate, but it violates the letter of the franchises of most of the companies. To this bill of claims will also be added the losses incident to carrying out the orders of our Department of State for all Americans to withdraw from Mexico on two occasions. Each time about one month's production was lost.

I have noted above the far-reaching possibilities of destruction to oil properties entailed in the "nationalization" plans. While these are in abeyance pending "investigation and legislation" the oil companies have other drains on their resources, such as government levies for dredging the river at Tampico (while the companies' own dredges do the work), the requirement of special licenses to drill each well, and the virtual curtailment of all development work outside the Tampico-Tuxpam district. All add to the total loot of the revolutionists, and continue the threat against foreign business development throughout all Mexico.

About $200,000,000 of American money has gone into mining in Mexico. Practically all of it has been legitimate business investment, in low grade or old abandoned bonanza properties, in mills and in smelters—the speculative period of bonanza mining such as we have had in our own West was passed in Mexico a century before American money began to flow across the Rio Grande. Our American investment could therefore by no means be regarded as a speculative venture, and the margin of return was relatively small—so small in fact that Mexicans did not and would not now consider such mining as profitable investment. We are, therefore, justified in taking a serious and calculating view of the damage done to American mining properties under revolutionary rule.

From sources available, I would estimate the damage done American mining properties in Mexico at $15,000,000—this is very conservative. There has, however, been little of the wanton destruction of mines such as the Germans practiced in Northern France. One instance, however, stands out, and this was to a coal mining property in northern Mexico, the Agujita, less than 100 miles south of Eagle Pass, Texas. In May, 1913, General Jesus Carranza, brother of the president, demanded $50,000 from the manager of this property, owned by American and other foreign capital. The money was not on the ground and there was no telegraphic communication with Mexico City, so it could not be paid. The property was then wrecked by Carranza soldiers, several hundred coke ovens blown up, the mines fired and flooded, buildings burned, etc.,—damage estimated at $1,000,000.

Some other incidents of this sort are recorded, but the largest physical damage is indirect, due to the driving off of workers and the murder of the American engineers, so that great mining properties were abandoned temporarily with the result that the water came in and tremendous values in timbering and stoping have been destroyed. In some instances the damage caused by water has mounted up to vast sums; one great mine, the Tiro General, an American property, will for instance require $300,000 before it can be operated again. Other properties abandoned from time to time during the years when railway traffic was interrupted, have similar bills for repairs, and hundreds of other mines, great and small, have been kept closed through the most profitable period mining has ever known (that during the Great War), with vast losses, although the ore is of course still in the ground and will some day be taken out.

The decrees and laws put into effect by the Mexican government in its effort to raise money have had a serious effect on mining. There have been new export taxes on metals, for instance, 5 per cent on lead, copper and zinc, where before nothing was assessed, and in some cases, as in that of copper, definite sums per pound have been assessed, with the result that the falling copper prices caused the closing of great properties like that of Cananea (American) and El Boleo (largely French). Silver and gold were taxed 10 per cent as against 2½ per cent in the old days; during the war the export of gold was prohibited and half of the value of the silver exported had to be returned to Mexico in gold. Taxes on mining claims also have been increased tremendously, so that in 1916 a group of forty-five American companies estimated for the American-Mexican commission sitting in Atlantic City that where in 1912 they paid $96,000 in taxes on a group of claims the new laws would have collected $569,000 and where in 1912 the export taxes were $1,726,000, the export taxes on the same quantity of metal (if it had been taken out, which it was not) would have been $7,000,000.

During the war, only high metal prices kept any mining business going in Mexico. After the armistice, hundreds of mines and all but a few smelters were closed down, and only the high price of silver, as long as it continued, allowed those that were left to keep running. Even during the era of high prices it was impossible for the mines which were operating to do the development work which alone makes possible the continued operation of mines under modern conditions.

Due to taxation, heavy freight costs, scarcity of materials and of labor, bandit raids and uncertain supplies, the science of mining in Mexico thus slipped back thirty years. This, in a phrase, sums up the reason for the losses and the conditions which make it impossible for mines to operate to-day where in times of ordered, intelligent government, they were running and supporting hundreds of thousands of Mexicans in comfort and peace.

Figures presenting the case of the land and cattle companies are almost impossible to obtain, for these interests have never organized as the oil and mining men have, and the only possible sources of such information have not been able to collect figures enough to cover the situation. Roughly, however, it is estimated that $50,000,000 of actual American money has been invested in land in Mexico, and although the titles to the properties still remain (always subject to the proposed confiscation of foreign property), the loss in capital invested, of live stock and crops, can probably be placed at over $10,000,000. The land companies and individual American holders of lands have, however, been the greatest sufferers, perhaps, of all the interests, for the actual worth of the land they occupied was infinitesimal compared with the value which their very presence and industry created for it.

The Mormon colonies of northern Chihuahua, near Casas Grandes, were amongst the most prosperous, in a comparatively large way, of all the agricultural sections of Mexico. Here the "desert blossomed as the rose" and the American colonists, industrious and prosperous, were becoming valuable contributors to the Mexican national wealth. All this has been swept away, houses burned, cattle run off, men, women and even the children murdered and maltreated, and the whole enterprise all but destroyed. The case is paralleled all over the country.

Millions of dollars have been invested by Americans in tropical plantations, and some at least of the properties were of great potential value. The story of the wrecking, raiding, pillaging and murdering on these properties would cover pages and the sums actually lost and the values destroyed by the interruption of development run up into great totals.

At the other end of the country, in Sonora, the records show the systematic ruin of the Yaqui Delta Land and Water Co., which, beginning under President Madero, had invested $3,000,000 in land, surveys and experiment stations and was turning a great property worthless for anything but grazing, into a paradise of irrigated farms. Beginning with Carranza and continuing steadily since this company's property has been despoiled, and by means of confiscatory legislation, new interpretations of franchises and overwhelming taxation has been reduced to ruin and even the government franchise itself finally annulled. The Mexicans have no plans and no money to do such vast development themselves, so the destruction of this property, pushing it back to the mere value of the grazing land, was utterly wanton and deprives Mexico of a great agricultural development of the type which she sorely needs.

In industrial, public service, banks and other classes of investment American money has been put into Mexico to a total of about $50,000,000. Most of the industrial and public service corporations are owned by foreigners in Mexico, the only exceptions being a few manufacturing plants and undeveloped tramway and city water plants. The majority of this capital is, however, British, French and German, American money having gone into the other interests described. Much of this industrial property has been destroyed, and the public service corporations have been taken over by the government on various pretexts and without payment, for the money they have earned has gone into the Mexican national war chest. There remains, however, the possibility of damage claims, which in these cases can be easily established.

Of the American corporations engaged in industries a typical case is that of the Continental Rubber Company, which has invested $5,000,000 in the guayule rubber business in north central Mexico. In 1910 the guayule exports of Mexico were 28,000,000 pounds, worth in the market approximately $20,000,000, and of this the Continental exported the largest share. To-day the guayule exports are practically nothing on the part of the companies, while the guayule shrubs on their lands are being cut and shipped by roving bands of bandits and peons. The vast Hacienda de Cedros, covering 2,000,000 acres, was bought by the company nearly fifteen years ago, when its value was around $1,000,000. At the height of the guayule business its worth was many times this sum, but to-day, even with the chances of a future recognition of the title of the American company, it could not be sold for its original cost. Like all foreign properties in Mexico which have been successful, the value of this hacienda was in the industry of the Americans who owned and managed it—a value which cannot be estimated or set down in figures in a damage claim.

The Mexican Banks of Issue, the backbone of the credit system of Mexico, were owned only in small part by American interests. Their destruction and the wiping out of the entire Mexican financial system which was built up by Diaz, must not be forgotten in trying to get a picture of the destruction wrought by the Mexican revolutionary bandits and their governments. The paper money systems which scourged the country from 1913 to 1916 cost foreigners millions of dollars which can never be shown in figures, owing to the fluctuations of the paper pesos. The upsetting of credit, which those who study the situation soon find was due largely to Carranza decrees (whether justified by circumstances or not) has set Mexico back nearly fifty years and has depressed values of property and investment beyond any calculation but the most careful studies by experts in finance as well as industry.

It is such phases of the Mexican credit system of to-day which constitute the real damage claims against Mexico—claims which can hardly be estimated. I place the figure at $1,000,000,000, and yet its potentialities are far more than that. At the present moment the greatest actual loss—even though it can be partially repaired if the future develops sane government in Mexico—is in the virtual destruction of the market for property in Mexico. The new constitution and the decrees and laws under it virtually prohibit foreigners from owning anything in a vast restricted zone along the border and seacoast, a zone including the richest foreign holdings in Mexico. They prohibit foreigners from owning real estate anywhere unless they agree never to appeal to their home governments in case of trouble. The effect of this is to eliminate the only possible market for valuable property. The Mexicans, and particularly the Mexicans who are in control to-day, will not, need not, can not buy such properties—foreigners and the opportunities which were open to foreigners in Mexico before the revolution actually created the market value of such property, because they and they alone were the possible purchasers.

Even well-developed small farming tracts cannot be sold to small Mexican farmers—such small farmers hardly exist as a class and where they do exist, their experience and their financial capacity do not lead them to consider the purchase of improved farms. And above all is the promise and the performance, in some cases, of the much-heralded land distribution of the revolutionary governments. Where men can get something for nothing, or on their own worthless credit, they do not buy in the open market.

Aside from this destruction of the values of foreign property holdings in Mexico by making transfer virtually impossible, there is, once more, that omnipresent menace of confiscation which makes men seek privileges instead of their as yet uncertain legal rights, for the protection of what they have. No longer do men buy to develop—they take, as in the oil fields, only what is sure to return large profits in a very brief time, for they know that even if they have privilege, and think they know how to keep on having privilege for themselves, they cannot transfer their capacity for getting privilege when they seek to sell their property. There are no longer relative values of property, in Mexico—property is worth only what can be got out of it, and got quickly.

This all makes up an uninspiring picture. But we must look on such pictures, must weigh and judge them ere we can see the way through and beyond them. That there is such a way must not be forgotten. It lies beyond the realm of mere political reform, for to-day, as all through the revolutionary history of Mexico the curse of the country is *the application of political remedies to economic ills*—that phrase should be burned into the brain of all who seek knowledge of the real Mexico.

That the relief is to come from the womb of revolution has been the hope of all who have watched the struggles in Mexico without understanding them. The failure of their hopes has been continuous. Madero, Huerta, Carranza, de la Huerta, Obregon,—to each in turn have such watchers transferred their allegiance and their faith. Each has failed, in so far as each has applied only the political remedy. The result has been the utter debasement of Mexican credit, the utter outraging of Mexican and foreign faith in Mexico herself. To-day, as I have said, Mexicans do not believe in Mexico, and each new failure of the political remedy sends them further away from her altars. What, then, is the answer?

The answer is but the following of the inexorable logic of life—and of business. We shall find it, not in the application of new politics, of new (or of old) constitutions and laws and decrees, not in the ravings of dreamers or of petty states-men. We shall find it, and shall know it when we find it, in a solution of the practical problems of Mexican commerce, labor and business by the practical men of affairs of Mexico and of the world. Our part shall be a very great part, for the business men of the United States, above all others, must show the way. Mexico must in the end bow to practical ideas of practical men, and in bowing to that yoke she will see her future unfold. Of the ways of finding the road and of turning Mexico upon it, we shall deal later. Only here, at the end of this dismal chapter of failure to solve the economic problems by political nostrums, I wish to indicate that there is, and will be, a way of hope and of salvation—from within Mexico herself.

CHAPTER VI
MEXICO AND HER "BOLSHEVISM"

Ten years ago Mexico was one of the great, progressive nations of the world; to-day she is just "another Latin American Republic." Then she showed literally the achievement and the promise of Japan; to-day she is as backward and as hopeless as Turkey. Ten years ago her diplomats were honored in the councils of kings, her credit ranked with that of the best of Europe, her cities were miniatures of Paris, her mines operated with the perfection of those in England, her railways and budding industries bore comparison with those of the United States, her people lived in arcadian peace, wakening slowly and surely, if sometimes painfully, to a civilization which was meeting their needs. To-day, Mexico is a little worse than Turkey, a little better than Hayti, her diplomats are as inconsequential as those of Thibet, her credit is as low as that of Austria, her cities and ports are mud puddles and pest holes, her mines are back to the rat-hole workings of the colonial Spaniards and Indians, her railroads are rattling skeletons, her industries virtually non-existent. Life is again arcadian, with all those discomforts of Arcadia which the poets of old and the propagandists of to-day neglect, so carefully, to mention.

The world has learned, in these past years, to take colossal destructions calmly, so that few of us wonder and none of us really questions the fact or the why of Mexico's sudden and astounding degeneration. And yet that failure is in miniature the threat and the promise of the failure of our civilization, in epitome the boast of bolshevism and the nightmare of capitalism. Mexico is like the Chamber of Horrors at the old Eden Musee or Mme. Tussaud's, a row of illuminated pictures which tell in ghastly realism what is sure to happen to careless people if they play too recklessly with the world which is given them to use.

This seems indeed a cycle of bolshevism, but it is a cycle in which radicalism, like capitalism, is a sorry victim. As a picture the events in Mexico approximate the drama in Russia, carried to the logical conclusions which such a drama would reach on any national stage where personal aggrandizement is a mightier lodestone than public devotion. The historical facts of the past decade in Mexico are unrelated to the facts and background of Russia, yet in Mexico there have been heard the same shibboleths, the same promises, the same cries of the downtrodden. There have been seen the same red flags, the same uprisings and assassinations, and the same "redistribution" of property as in Russia. And more than all has unrolled the drama of the rising of obscure chieftains and politicians to colossal and wicked power. But in Mexico the cycle has gone far beyond Russia, perhaps because here there has, indeed, been no touch of even such idealism as there may be in Moscow.

In Mexico the crimson day of bolshevism has been followed quickly by the purple twilight of the aftermath of graft and privilege. To-day there is to be seen there a power of wealth mightier than any which is conceivable in the now almost forgotten dawn of bolshevism's red day in Mexico. Privilege and not the proletariat, capitalism and not socialism, are the gods of that stricken land,—a land which ten years ago was mistress of her life and of her destiny, and to-day is a beggar in the marts of the world, ready to sell her body and her soul for gold.

I have no desire to force a parallel between the early events in Mexico and those in Russia. The parallel is there, and could fill the eye and mind with the aid of a modicum of imagination. But the facts alone are eloquent, and the primary fact is not whether the revolution against the czar was day for day and hour for hour a repetition of the Madero revolution against Diaz, or whether Huerta was an Indian Denekin, or Carranza a weak Lenin or Obregon the realization of what Trotzky might be to-morrow or next year. The first fact and the last is that in one great section of Mexico we have seen and in the whole of Mexico we are to-day watching the rolling on of an ugly spiral from plutocracy to revolution, from revolution to socialism, from socialism to bolshevism and then from bolshevism to demagogy, to a later and darker dictatorship, with a more miserable proletariat, and on into the vast sweep of an age of privilege which holds and wields power greater than government, greater and more direct than capital or labor has ever wielded. For privilege stands alone in the midst of the smoking ruins of what was once the Mexican nation.

He braves much in this day who dares define or limit bolshevism, but in Mexico its manifestations have been carried to a point where they have limited and defined themselves. First, Mexican bolshevism was and is the application of political remedies to economic ills; second, it is the raising up of the proletariat by promises and agitation to the overturning of established government and the setting up, not of the promised millennium, but of new dictatorships and new oppressions. Both sought, and claim, the improvement of the workers, but both have failed and faded to shadowy appearance and raucous boast.

In Mexico to-day there are spots where peace and progress reign—but they are literally those spots where "capitalism," entrenched behind a wall of gold and foreign protection, has been able to give its workers the value of the profits which they gain. The rest of Mexico is worse off, politically and economically, than in the days of Diaz, and increasingly the only hope of the country seems, by some means, to achieve the extension of sane business to the replacement of the economic ruin of native demagogues masquerading behind the fair words of socialism.

The essence of the beneficent effects of this foreign business has been the education of the Mexicans whom it touches toward broader horizons of living and personal efficiency. For actually the history of Mexico's downfall is a history of the failure of her education, of the failure of the past governments of Mexico to utilize the forces which were at their hand for the uplift and the development of the unhappy masses of the people. That failure of the past has become a colossal catastrophe in the days of present and past revolution.

For their day and time, Spain and the Roman Catholic church did much for Mexico. We do not know what the Church might have done if it had had different, more educational ideals, but we do know that, save for the work of the Protestant missions in the past thirty years, hardly any other force but Rome has done anything for social improvement in Mexico. We do not know what Anglo-Saxon educational and economic leadership would have done in the place of that of the Spaniards and mixed-bloods—such comparisons are necessarily academic. But we do know that under the Spanish viceroys and under Diaz more was done toward improving the material welfare and toward building the foundations of material and moral prosperity for the unfortunate peons than has been done or even sincerely attempted in the ten years of revolutionary rule since the fall of Diaz.

Mexico has been, and indeed is, what we sometimes call in our brusque Americanism, a "white man's country." It is essentially one of the spots in this world where the burden of uplift is the white man's burden. For 300 years white Spaniards sought to lift it, and in that long effort, with all its failures, they placed Mexico, even with her six millions of unlettered, superstitious Indians, in the category of the white lands. The duty of the white man, imperialist or socialist as he may be, has ever been two-fold, and its duality has been its power; we have lifted the material plane of our wards and we have upraised those wards themselves to a higher and yet higher mental and spiritual plane.

It is this dual duty that the revolutionists of Mexico have shirked and have scouted. The economic rain of the country is to-day almost complete, and its spiritual uplift has been halted as by a wall of flame. From those material ruins, Mexico might conceivably rise in a spiritual rebirth, but the fact has been otherwise, for the material ruin has been accomplished by the prostitution of all the ideals, all the sacred faiths of men, concentrated by self-seeking bandit governments to the aggrandizement and the enrichment of a few sodden favorites.

I would, if I could, paint a different picture, but the half lights of such a panorama can be added only after the dull background has been set in. And that background is dark indeed. The panorama of misery begins when one crosses the northern border to-day. There the scattered but once almost happy villages of other times have been replaced by ruined, roofless railway stations lined with starving vendors of food who fight with the bony dogs for the refuse of the very food they sell. All the long trip to Mexico City is marked by the same voiceless suffering, and the capital itself has a dismal dinginess that cries of hopeless misery, in appalling contrast to the gallant days of the Diaz "materialism."

The unhappy toll of war and revolution, one says? Yes, in part, for such "war" as Mexico has known always takes that toll and always, too, from the weaklings, putting starvation and sickness and filth and dismay where once were comfort and health and some cleanliness and happiness.

But, again the question, was it not worth the price, will it not be worth the price, in the victories won for human freedom? And here the answer is unequivocably "No."

Many hoped, with the fine faith of their own sincerity, that the upheaval which followed Diaz was the dawning of a new era. But in that hope even those who knew Mexico forgot the Mexicans and their history. Political independence from Spain had been won, freedom from the domination of religious bigotry had been won, before Diaz came. The struggle of his day was one of uplift, carried on with faulty tools, perhaps, but slowly reaching toward the light. Living was improving, slowly; religion was improving, slowly; education was advancing, slowly. Then came a period of crystallization; the Diaz oligarchy grew old. Many sincere men, inside and outside Mexico, thought that the advance could and should move more rapidly. Diaz repressed those hastening reformers, and the spiritual force which finally broke forth into the Madero revolution of 1910-11 was undoubtedly the result of that repression of progressive thought.

Like all the revolutions of Mexico's stormy history, this one began with a beautiful stating of ideals and of the unrealized needs of the common man; but as with all those other revolutions, the power passed quickly to the hands of men whose sole "ideal" was personal aggrandizement, personal wealth, and ruin to all whose needs might incommode these exalted "leaders."

The so-called "social revolution" of Mexico borrowed the battle cries of European socialism, but in the land in which it worked it stirred up only a tempest in a teapot, with the miserable masses of the country serving as tinder and fuel beneath the vessel. The teapot is the diminutive organized labor world of Mexico, and that is boiling more violently, perhaps, than elsewhere. But to-day the "advanced" ideas of Mexico serve, in the name of socialism, only to put sweeping power into the hands of unscrupulous men, men who know and care nothing of the responsibilities of power, and are using it only to the destruction of the very bases of Mexican society.

Thus, while there seems to be a light dawning in the labor world of Mexico, I am not sure that the light does not come from the burning of something which Mexico cannot afford to lose. In that organized labor world there are fewer than 50,000 workers out of a population of 15,000,000, while there are more than 3,000,000 peons, heads of families, who work, when there is work, in the fields, or as common laborers. It is upon the continued, unbroken suffering of these 3,000,000 that the 50,000 profit to-day—the peons have but changed masters once again and in the name of freedom, now, serve a vaster company. The Mexican leaders, drawing their power in turn from the coherent, organized industrial workers, are to-day destroying the civilization of Diaz, and with it the civilization of American business men, American teachers and American missionaries, which was and is the hope of the downtrodden majority. The "modern" laws which labor has promulgated might, we may conceive, fit the advanced industrial life of Germany or the United States, but they are utterly suicidal to Mexico. The new Constitution of 1917 has written into its fabric an idealistic set of labor laws, beautiful in terminology but under present conditions of industry and psychology and government in Mexico, about as impractical for the development of industry and the true welfare of labor as they are efficient as a means of graft and extortion against labor as well as against employers. These laws are worked out for the sole benefit of the industrial workers of Mexico, that total of less than 50,000 as against the 3,000,000 farm and day laborers. They are thus far more important as a propaganda document with the foreign radicals who caused the inclusion of those administrative laws in the new national constitution than they are helpful to Mexico's own social advancement.

The eight-hour day provided in the constitution, the welfare projects such as the stern proviso that nursing mothers shall have two half-hour periods per day in which to care for their children, the constitutional support of the right to strike even in public utilities, and the virtual provision against the employment of strikebreakers, or the closing of a shop in a lock-out, are typical of the privileges for labor—they cover everything which the most radical would make the laws of every land. In Mexico, and under the peculiar conditions of Mexican psychology and inter-class relationships, they become little more than tools of the demagogues. The rulers do as they choose in any case, as when, not long ago, a railway strike was successful to the last detail of the demands made in the name of "the social revolution" and two months later a similar strike for similar ends was opposed by the general use of strikebreakers. The labor courts, theoretically a great advance, are used almost without exception as a palladium of radical propaganda—and as a toll-gate on the road of privilege.

Such are the reforms of the new era. They provide six or eight hour days, for men who cannot read and whose children are not taught to read or to think. They provide minimum wages, to be determined by factory committees, with the most ignorant workmen in the world on a par with employers and industrial engineers. They provide against discharge for any cause except proven drunkenness, in a land where, to say the least, drunkenness is relative.

Their own people have begun, a little, to wonder at the wisdom of these sweeping changes, and one, Ing. Carlos Arroyo, not long ago wrote in the official but very radical "Bulletin of Industry, Commerce and Labor" that there were four main difficulties which would have to be corrected before factory efficiency could be arranged in Mexico on a coöperative basis: first, scientific method would have to replace the empirical system now in use; second, there would have to be special training for apprentices; third, there would have to be study of employees to have them properly placed; fourth, the responsibility for the tasks assigned would have to be "equally" divided (not given entirely to the workers) between the management and the workers, "because the former continues to be charged with the responsibility for the competence of the latter."

And as to that competence, this same bulletin regularly publishes the records of accidents. There one will find that in 1918, for instance, there were, in 278 industrial establishments having 292,364 employees, 6,424 accidents, in which 184 were killed, and 42 maimed and 6,198 wounded. And, most illuminating of all, 5,165 of the accidents were admittedly due to the "carelessness of workmen," only 195 were the fault of the management and 1,064 were due to unavoidable causes.

As to the value of the achieved reforms, I have but this to tell: In all the cities, in the centers of industry like the Tampico oil fields and the busy port of Vera Cruz (busier to-day than it has ever been because all Mexico must live on imported goods) I found a sullen hatred of the foreigner, an ugly self-assertion that bodes but ill for those missionaries of religion and of business to whom we look for so much of the future regeneration of the country. I saw none of the contented, happy calm of prosperous laborers, but only the unrest of the great cities of other lands, ugly with resentment, fertile field for revolution but not for progress. And yet those very resentful workers, convinced of an unappreciated importance which they knew but by rote, are all that there is of the "fruits" of the "social revolution" in Mexico.

No, Mexico has not changed, even amongst her petted laboring classes, and I fear that the old rule of our ancient civilization will have to persist a little longer, and the long, dim road be trod again through failure and reform, and failure again and yet again. I fear that we shall still have to lift by reaching down and, by training the dull forces of those dull minds, teach them to help themselves and to climb by themselves.

Out on the plantations the workers are going the rounds which they have covered since Mexico began, and in the fairs I saw the only evidence of happiness which smile on one in the length and breadth of the country. The market places and the fairs of Mexico, sunny, crowded, colorful, rich because the Indians in the booths are close to Nature and Nature's bounty! That simple happiness has been the source of all Mexico's joy—and of all her misfortune. That simplicity has made her people the dupes of predatory chieftains, and hideous priests of pre-Spanish times, of Spaniard and priest through the long centuries of the viceroys, of master and of some priests, too, through the years since the Independence. Yet in those periods those who have duped the Indians have, most of them, protected the Indians in an easy, medieval way, and slowly there has grown a civilization, and in that civilization have been nurtured the seeds of better things.

The time was coming for those seeds to bear fruit, when, hastening the ripening, came the revolutions of 1910 and after. It was like the child who pulled up the stalks to see how the seeds were growing—they were growing much faster than appeared on the surface, but they did not grow after they were pulled up.

Looking back to the Diaz day we can find, for instance, the slow, constructive work toward the creation of arable land for small farms. It was being hampered somewhat by grasping office-holders, but it was advancing, a great national plan of irrigation to make possible the use of small tracts in a country where rain conditions have forever made small farming all but impossible. Then the revolution and the resounding cry for "land." The alleged land hunger of the Mexican Indians and peons has been at once the rallying cry for each succeeding revolution and the one appeal of all of them for foreign sympathy.

But whatever authorities may conceive as to the facts of the existence of this land hunger or of the forms which it takes—a desire for little farms, for prehistoric communal ownership, or for property only because it is wealth and can be converted into cash—it is also true that the schemes of the revolutionists for land distribution have been impossible except by the confiscation of rich properties and the destruction of vested rights. Obviously, no land which is not tillable is satisfactory for distribution, and the tillable land of Mexico is, as I have pointed out, actually only about 25,000,000 acres, or one-twentieth of the area of the country. Land distribution must long remain largely a beautiful theory, good only for raising up the natives by direct appeal to their bitter poverty or to their human greed, and for the raising up of foreign sympathy by the flaunting of the misfortunes of the soil under more appealing names.

In Mexico to-day all these dreams of land distribution have gone the way of other "reforms" for the benefit of the peons. Nothing, virtually, has been done. Some great properties have been confiscated, or "paid for" in unguaranteed bonds of bankrupt state governments, but most of such properties are to-day in the hands of former revolutionary "generals." Some few have been distributed to Indians, but even these tracts are taken with but scant enthusiasm. One great "land distribution" in Yucatan called forth a crowd of 6,000 to the festival (all Mexico goes to any *fiesta*) but only thirty Indians took up any of the hundreds of small tracts offered.

The essential facts of the Mexican situation are patent to all who go to Mexico to-day, and they are inescapable to those who have a background of knowledge of Mexico by which to judge of what they see. And yet it is true that in the councils of Carranza, in the entourages of de la Huerta and of Obregon there have been men representing forces which we in our time have felt could not be used to evil purpose. These were men who had been stirred by the fine frenzy of the first revolution, and whose ideas, caught as mere phrases by the leaders of revolts, were handed back to their originators again, as the "ideals" of the revolution. Strange indeed it is, and yet not only newcomers, but foreigners of long residence and sincere and devoted Mexicans as well, fell victims to that subtle flattery. In business, in education, in the churches, there were such men, their very hopes too great to protect them from the petty deceits of those who climbed to power upon them.

I think I can understand why travelers in Mexico, sincere students as well as moistily entertained excursions of American "Chambers of Commerce" can be deceived as to conditions there. I have been inclined to be impatient with those who let themselves be led this way and that, and flattered by the apparent sincerity of self-deluding Mexican officials, but Mexico is, after all, an eternal enigma. It is an enigma because its colossal depths of ignorance and the smallness of its deceits are literally incomprehensible to simpler and less subtle minds.

It is that enigma which I have sought through all my writing on Mexico to resolve. On my last trip through the country, I saw just the eternal Mexico, the Mexico of ignorance and misery, whose only change was that it was a little sadder, a little more resentful of those whom it once regarded as its helpers and its friends, a little more pompous in parading its borrowed intellectual plumage.

A most perfect example of this ability of the Mexican of the "modern" type to absorb one's ideas and deceive one by the redishing of those ideas, happened to me on my last trip to Mexico City. In the course of the preparation of an article on a great business for a popular magazine, I met a Mexican *licenciado* (a title of vast elegance, meaning much more than its dictionary equivalent of "lawyer") who was extremely anxious to be quoted as an expert on the subject which I was studying. He evidently thought that my quoting him would help him to a government post to which he aspired, so he expounded his ideas at great length. When he was finished, I answered his arguments in kind, and with considerable interest in his response to my counter-play. He was pleasantly combative, and we parted in thorough friendship.

It was only a few hours later that I had an urgent call from this same gentleman, who had, he told me, been going into new material on the subject, and wished to express his views, stated in the morning, more definitely to me. Whereupon he returned me, recooked and eloquently served, my own friendly contentions of the previous interview. It was a bit thick for me, but it is worth the telling that an American business man of long experience in Mexico who had introduced this gentleman to me remarked when the subject came up again, a day or two later:

"By the way, Licenciado Blank is getting much broader. He has figured out a pretty decent attitude on this problem ..." and he redished me my own views again!

This is Mexico to-day. On the top a group of men who have absorbed in just this way the phrases of the intelligent radicals of the world but who still remain, as always, sycophants without background of education, or even genuine radical convictions. Below them the vast misery of the unthinking serfs of the country, duller, certainly sadder and even less well nourished than in the days of the viceroys and of Diaz.

We are all responsible for the Mexico which is before us. We Americans of every type in that old Mexico were too willing to let the misery of Mexico be what it was, were too willing to take our helpers and our support from the middle classes which were emerging so slowly. We made a fetish of that middle class, built our hope of Mexico upon it, called it the crowning achievement of the age of Diaz, and from it came the beginnings of that group of Mexican leaders of which we all had dreamed. We saw Diaz clear—all of us, I think—and knew that his day could not be forever. But we had faith in that middle class, forgetting, as it was easy to forget, the instability of that foundation of Indian poverty and misery. We were going to transmute those shifting sands by making more striking the examples of its brothers—artisans and clerks and students and teachers. We trusted so blindly, then, in the leaven of example—we knew so little of the sodden flour which made our loaves.

And then came the day of revolution, Madero the deliverer. There were few of us who regretted the passing of Diaz, save sentimentally, that it should have to be in just that way—we had hoped he would die gloriously, beloved by the people for whom he had given so much. And then the disappointment and the horror of that wild cabal of graft and loot under Madero, when the dreamers, the repressed brains of a generation, stood waiting, wringing their hands in helpless impotence—those who could, truly, have done so much! It was pitiful, as was the aftermath of Huerta, the reaction, the impossible reaction with its ugly tinge of a coming uprush of Indian barbarism.

Then Carranza, riding upon the winged horse of Madero—it seems that not all of us understood, quite, for we heard the fair words, as we have heard them echoing through empty halls and across dead and tortured bodies these five years since. Many sincere men were caught by those fair, echoing words, and many followed the phantom to the end. And many continue to this day.

I have no need to talk of the recent past, nor of the present. The story is written in the starving babies of the Mexican towns, in the dismal railway stations where wretched food can be bought (if one dares) from the very mouths of hungry, filthy vendors. Misery and grief and pain stalk in Mexico to-day. Somewhere those who have used these wretched bodies, as infinite in number, as minute in importance, as the skeletons of a coral reef, for climbing to wealth and power—somewhere these must make answer.

In another chapter I shall tell something of the story of Yucatan, where the ideas of radical socialism were accepted and then used to destroy even itself. It is a story of horror and of wreckage, the clearest picture of Mexican conditions at their ultimate which has passed in the gory panorama of the recent years.

What has happened in Yucatan is in essence what has been going on all over Mexico. In the larger field of the whole country, the revolutionists have been more coherent, and at the same time in their utterances somewhat more considerate of the prejudices of the world at large. Yucatan, isolated from the rest of Mexico, and free from the prying eyes of most of the world as well, has gone on with the round of despotism and oppression, rape and murder in the name of socialism, but on the mainland, the "rights of labor" have been more elaborately defended (in words) and the legal systems of confiscation and anti-foreignism have been more logically developed, under the standard of progressive socialism!

The years have written records of Mexican political and social revolution which are identical with those of the present in all save their battlecries. The first outbreak against Spain in 1810 and the dozens of revolutions which followed it were a *reductio ad absurdum* of the political ideals of Thomas Paine and the American and French revolutionaries. The Constitution of 1857, under which Diaz ruled, was little more than a copy of the Constitution of the United States, and few of its provisions were really adapted to Mexico's peculiar conditions. So it is not strange, perhaps, that the Constitution of 1917 is as far from being Mexican and far more false an effort to solve the nation's problems than was its predecessor, for it was dictated by foreign radicals and merely adapted by the Mexican politicians who knew best what would arouse enthusiasm in the Mexican crowd.

Despite its beauties of theory and its direct appeal to the serious radical thought of the world, its most useful function is becoming obvious even to the most credulous, for it gives the governing groups that control of Mexican life by which it is possible for them to sell the privilege of doing business, because the ancient rights of business are utterly done away with. The ills of Mexico are essentially economic, and the new constitution and its revolutions, even more than their predecessors, have sought to apply only the political remedy, a remedy which has so far served only to destroy the efficiency of the economic machinery of the country and place it upon the auction-block of graft.

To-day all over Mexico, labor is paid higher wages than it ever received, but it is paying more for its food and shelter than it ever spent before. The misery of Mexico is just as obvious and as unescapable as ever to him who sees truly. Save for those sections where foreign business still survives the Mexican lives as he has always lived, on the verge of pauperism. And upon the summit of the heap, lounging in easy magnificence, is the mixed-blood agitator, the general, the governor, the cabinet official who have battened on Mexico's misery before this day and will doubtless do so long after this day is passed.

The raising of the Indian masses of Mexico by promises and by high-sounding battlecries is a game as old as Mexican history; it is played with unvarying success year after year and generation after generation. The more extravagant the promises, the more complete the enthusiasm of the "proletariat," both for the political movement of the moment, and for the one which follows it immediately upon the discovery by the unfortunate "people" that the previous promises are not going to be kept.

But in to-day's orgy of revolution, Mexico has gone further toward destruction than she has ever gone before. Values throughout native Mexico are almost non-existent, and the wheels of Mexican civilization like the wheels of the wheezy locomotives of her railways, creak and groan on their rounds. The nation's economic life is tied together by strings, and what remains is only what has been salvaged from her junk-heaps, and like the lawn-mower borrowed from a neighbor, is kept running only to serve the purposes of the borrower.

The seventy years of warfare before Diaz left intact the civilization of the Spaniards for Diaz to revive, but the ten years from Diaz to Obregon have torn that civilization to shreds. Nearly all that Diaz built has disappeared, and to-day the business of Mexico is swapping jack-knives and selling food and shelter at the highest prices the traffic will bear.

No man who would face truth in Mexico can ignore these potent facts. And the reason is not revolution, nor even mere radicalism, but the cynical application of political control to economic needs for the aggrandizement of individual leaders whose power is in the market for all who will buy the privileges which they have to offer.

It is in this condition that the importance and the menace of radical Mexican government are found. What it has seemed well to call bolshevism in Mexico has its greatest power in its mere threat against capital and business. That threat, the mere presence of the anti-capitalistic constitution and laws, has probably far greater power than their actual application would have. Once the blow of confiscation fell, the answer from the world of business and civilized government would be quick and sure—Mexico cannot be ignored as Russia can be, for Mexico lies in the center of the trade-routes of the globe, and we in the United States would feel the menace of her anarchy too strongly to remain passive.

But the static power, the threat of laws which are never enforced—there is the menace and there the great influence which creates the graft and cynicism of Mexican officials. So long as those laws remain, business, if it would survive in Mexico, must buy immunity. And it does buy it, for business is ever timid, and no single business organization and seldom a group of business organizations, will ever go to the stake for a principle. Its duty to its stockholders and to its employees makes it buy its way, not always by direct graft, but in submission to vast taxes, to unwarranted extortions, to the riding of official annoyances—rather than accept the shut-down and fight with its own great power, its inertia of movement or of the silence which ruins empires.

In recent months the great business groups in Mexico have opposed a certain amount of strength to the growing power of the auction-block of Mexican graft and privilege. The oil companies have from time to time offered a solid front to the encroachments of this marketing of the privilege of doing business in contraversion of the temporary laws of Mexico. They have held back, apparently, the crushing fall of actual enforcement of the confiscatory provisions of the Constitution of 1917, and they have, here and there, stopped the marketing of privilege—for brief periods. But looking at the whole picture, it seems as if the Mexican officials of the present era are in no greater hurry to enforce the confiscation than are the foreigners to have it enforced. The static power of those provisions, waiting to fall, is far more profitable to Mexican pockets than would be the sudden and final crash of their genuine application. Their enforcement would be of little value to the seller of privilege, for then he would have to invent another method of extortion. No, privilege will long remain upon the market counters of Mexico. It will remain there, in fact, until some means is found, within or without Mexico, for destroying the system which is so profitable. That need of change is the crisis of the business world of Mexico, the crisis of all who would do business with Mexico in the present or in the future.

What, then, can save Mexico in this crisis? The panacea of the Obregon idea was certainly not a solution. Here indeed was a probably genuine desire to solve the problem in a final and glorious way. But the tools were but the tools of the old days of Carranza and the rest. That was a political remedy for an economic condition, and its promise was a sordid thing, an unworthy thing for Mexico or for the United States to expect. For the promise of Obregon was at first for reaction, a belief that Obregon was comfortably wealthy already or that his ambition was for power alone. Therefore he was to be the great conservative, who would save Mexico by slipping back to the days of Diaz. But reaction must always fail in the end. In this case it passed quickly, for this was a "reaction" which was part and parcel of the "radicalism" of Carranza, its power but a manifestation in another form of the same personalism, the same sale of privilege, which made Carranza impossible and in the end, brought him to his ruin.

The later developments of the Obregon idea were marked by an obvious anxiety to reach a permanent solution of the immediate and pressing difficulties of Mexico, and most of all to secure recognition by the United States and financial aid from American bankers, as the *sine qua non* of such a solution. The efforts put forth were powerful, but the driving force back of them was primarily personal ambition and the realization that only such a solution could save the happy hunting grounds of revolutionary leaders from some sort of foreign intendancy. And above and beyond and behind all, were the factors of government whose origins and whose immediate past seem indeed to be as firmly stamped upon their natures as the spots upon the leopard or his skin upon the Ethiopian.

The completed cycle of the bolshevist experiment and the arrival back at the sale of privilege links up with the failure of Obregon to offer anything but, first, a promise of reversion to reactionary czarism and, second, that unconcealed offering of privileges and promises of power to all who could or who might aid in the campaign for recognition and for foreign loans. The condition seems to me to sound a call as of Elijah for a new understanding of the Mexican problem. Carrancism might have been but an isolated interlude, might have been a mere question of observation and interpretation, if the end had not come and if business in Mexico were not continuing to pay for its sorry privileges in the same sorry way. Obregon might perhaps have been the hope for peace and happiness in Mexico if we had not had Carranza and de la Huerta and if their followers, with their cynical mouthings of all the most sacred faiths of man, were not to-day still the rulers of Mexico, still the sellers of privilege in the name of human progress.

We must, I believe, cast away the too long nurtured idea that the battle in Mexico is between the progressive thought of the day and the reactionary conservatism of great interests. I have sought here to show why this is so. A revolution which can evolve the idea of the socialization of great industry and can, in the very conception of that idea, turn it to the looting of that industry for private graft and gain, as in Yucatan; a revolution which can produce the uncontrolled radicalism of Carranza and evolve through the cynical play-acting of de la Huerta into the promise of reactionism in Obregon with all the unholy forces which supported Carranza rallying to uphold his successors—such a revolution will not, unredeemed, carry Mexico into her next era of progress and peace. Capital and socialism must alike beware. Neither should, in honesty with itself, accept a cause in Mexico until the issue is joined clear.

In the past ten years we have seen in turn the appeal of political Mexico, to-day to the bolshevist, to-morrow to the Christian missionary, to-day to the thinking radical of the universities, to-morrow to the deep-dyed conservative of the counting room. Confusion has piled upon confusion until we have each seen in Mexico what we hoped or what we feared.

We can only begin to see the truth, and in the truth the solution of the complicated Mexican problem, when we clear our minds of these old ideas that he who is against the revolutionary government in Mexico is a hopeless reactionary, and that he who is for it is a raving bolshevist. For the Mexican revolution is part of the "world revolution" only as the shibboleths of that vast upheaval have been turned to the aggrandizement of Mexican leaders who know neither what the phrases mean nor where they lead.

If this is grasped, and if we will look at Mexico as a problem for us all, then the beginning of the road away from foreign intervention and the peril to our peace and Mexico's will begin to open. Intervention can be avoided, even though it may be grievously close to-day. But it cannot be avoided until we see clearly that the issue of intervention, like the whole issue of the Mexican revolution, is not one of capitalistic interests against the unhappy Mexican peon, but a struggle of all the constructive thinkers and workers of the world—be they radical, socialistic, religious, philosophical, laborite, capitalistic, industrial or social, be they American, English, French, Russian or Mexican—against forces of greed and ignorance which turn every ideal of honest men to the prostitution of their country and the exploitation of their fellows within and without its borders.

CHAPTER VII
THE RAPE OF YUCATAN

From the golden wheat fields of Kansas to the barren sands of Yucatan, from the loaf of bread on your table to the loot of Mexican revolutions—these seem mighty leaps of imagination or of fiction. Yet the link is closer than imagination could ever forge, the analogy a stranger tale than the yarns of Captain Kidd.

The modern industry of wheat farming depends, by one of the romantic balances of world commerce, upon the supply of binder twine for the mechanical harvester, a supply which comes alone, to-day, from the cultivation of a humble cactus plant in far-off Yucatan. The great Mexican industry of raising this henequen or sisal hemp was prostituted by Mexican revolutionists to the manipulation of the binder twine market so that in four years more than a hundred million dollars in artificially inflated prices were dragged from American farmers. Thus it was that through the helpless years of the Great War, all who ate the bread of the wheat, from you and me in America to the starving children of Belgium, paid bitter tribute to the greed of Mexican agitators.

The story of Yucatan is no mere tale of the by-play of revolution, the "fortunes of war" or the "necessary accompaniments of a great social upheaval." It is the history of the deliberate looting of a commonwealth and of an indispensable international industry. In the name of socialism, shouting the battle-cries of the age-long struggle for human freedom, Mexican revolutionary leaders turned the richest agricultural state of Mexico into a desert waste, prostituted the only creative industry in the whole country to the looting of the world's farmlands and the taxing of every loaf of bread consumed in the world. The vast tribute which thus poured into the coffers of revolutionary government was utterly lost to public vision almost before it had left the market-places, and not one cent of it was ever turned to the easing of the sorry human burden of the Mexican peon or devoted to the education and upbuilding of the Mexican people.

The story of Yucatan is the story of as gruesome a rape of Mother Earth as man has known. Beginning with the familiar picture of the downtrodden peon of the Diaz time, it runs the gamut through the marching armies of conquerors, through a cycle of high-sounding socialism to bloody oppressions, and on to a newer despotism and finally to utter economic collapse. In the end it flattens down into the present, an era of capitalistic struggle in which the state, by the laws of economics which its despots perverted so vigorously, is being ground between the millstones of opposing forces of the very business which was once the source of all its wealth and all its progress.

Upon the wheat crop of the world depends the life of the world, and upon the mechanical harvester depends, literally, the life of the modern wheat industry. In its turn, the operation of the harvester is dependent upon the millions of miles of binder twine which alone make possible the handling of the wheat on its way from the standing fields to the thresher which converts it to golden grain. Since Cyrus McCormick first offered his "reaper" to the American farmer, more than fifty years ago, invention has sought far and wide for freedom from the need of twine for the binding of the sheaves, but neither "header" nor mechanical flail has been able to achieve it; to-day the wheat farmer must have twine, and that by the hundreds and millions of pounds, to harvest his crop.

Thus, because the sisal hemp or henequen of Yucatan is the only fiber which can be produced in sufficient quantities at a low price to meet the farmer's need for binder twine, the wheat for the world's food supply depends vitally on the product of this one distant state of Mexico. Without its humble aid, the American farmer might, conceivably, hark back to the binding of wheat sheaves by hand—it is certain that we could anticipate the scrapping of billions of dollars' worth of mechanical harvesters in the substitution of some other method than theirs. The only other fiber that will serve for the making of binder twine is true Manila hemp, whose total crop would not fill a tenth of the needs of the world's annual harvest, and whose finer quality and greater cost have caused it to be devoted almost exclusively to the making of high-class cordage. Cotton and jute and silk and all other known or promised vegetable or animal fibers from which binder twine might conceivably be made have proven useless for the purpose. One of them is too stout, one too soft, one too short of fiber, one not brittle enough, another too brittle. Sisal, the Yucatan henequen, is to-day the only hemp which meets all demands of the world's annual wheat harvest, a demand which has reached the colossal total of 400,000,000 pounds a year.

Upon this need has been built the one great creative industry of Mexico, the one business, agricultural or manufacturing, which in Mexico produces wealth through human energy. Its source is the long-leaved henequen plant, to whose necessarily slow growth for fiber the sandy, desert soil of the Yucatan coastland is peculiarly adapted. The henequen is a species of the great agave, that strange, cactus-like "Century plant," which is found in one form or another in almost all desert countries. As the maguey, it grows in the great Central Mexican plateau, furnishing the heavy drink called *pulque*, and giving up a hand-extracted fiber which has been woven into the raiment of the Indians of the Valley of Mexico for centuries. Still other varieties, in the warmer sections of Mexico, furnish food for cattle and, distilled, the fiery *mescal* or *tequila* which is an even more terrible curse of Mexico than the much-berated *pulque*.

It is the henequen, however, which is the most commercially useful of all the agaves, for its narrow leaves, three to four feet long, are peculiarly adapted to the mechanical extraction of their fiber (which most of the agaves are not). The coarse, rasping, yellow strands have the thickness and the strength of horsehair, so that they survive the vigorous de-pulping process of the great gin-like machines. After drying, they furnish a stout fiber which, when woven into thick cord, ties the wheat sheaves in the harvester, and breaks easily as each sheaf is thrown back into the thresher in the gorgeous pageant of the harvest.

This henequen, the sisal hemp of commerce, was first exported in 1864, and by 1880 was one of the well-known but minor fibers in the American market. In 1898, when the Spanish-American war cut off the exports of Manila hemp, henequen sprang into immediate and great importance, its price rose from 2½ cents to 10 cents a pound in New York, and an immediate increase in the industry and in the economic importance of the state of Yucatan took place. There was a lively boom in henequen lands, and incidentally an improvement in social and political conditions in Yucatan, followed by something of a slump with a few mild panics around 1907.

But henequen fiber had been definitely established in the market and selling as it did at an average price of 5¼ cents a pound, became the great staple for the manufacture of binder twine. This new and virtually inexhaustible supply of cheap fiber for twine-making played its part in the broadening use of the mechanical harvester, until by 1915 Yucatan henequen binder twine was being shipped to every wheat producing area in the world, from the Siberian steppes to the pampas of the Argentine.

In 1914 the exports from Mexico were more than a million bales or approximately 400,000,000 pounds, which was a doubling of production in fourteen years. The current price of about 6 cents a pound had enabled the Yucatan growers to build up immense fortunes and made it possible for the manufacturers of the thousands of tons of binder twine to furnish it to the American farmer at less than 10 cents a pound.

The chief manufacturers of binder twine and, therefore, the chief buyers of Yucatan henequen, are the International Harvester Company, which makes about half the binder twine used in the world, the Plymouth Cordage Company, which makes about a quarter of the entire supply, and various state penitentiaries in the wheat belt of the United States. All of these manufacturers work on close margins for the Harvester Company's business is selling harvester machines and it seems interested materially in keeping the price of such accessories as twine as low as possible. The effect of this, combined with Yankee shrewdness, has been a continuous effort to keep the price of Yucatan henequen down to rock bottom, and to this end its buyers have been cheerful arbiters of the price of the sisal in the Mexican market.

They were never, however, quite the grasping, grinding capitalistic despots they were described as being by the Yucatecans, for those of us who can remember back into the philosophic days before 1914 will recollect that it was not customary for even American capital to kill the geese that laid the golden eggs. The Yucatan hacendados were encouraged to demand, and get, comfortable prices for their product, and incidentally to plant large new acreages of the henequen plants.

It was this large planting, which went on from 1900 to 1914, which caused the first glimmering of the idea of "direct action" on the part of the hacendados, the growers of the sisal. It takes seven years for henequen plants to come into bearing, and the prospect of immensely increased production and probably lowered prices inspired the first idea of a pool which would maintain the old price levels. In 1912 a scheme for regulating the price of henequen was first presented to his fellows by a Yucatan hacendado. His idea was not so much to create an artificial shortage by storing the hemp, as to form some sort of organization which would have first chance to buy the henequen crop and thus make the hacendados participants in the profits made by the jobbers or middlemen.

The organization which resulted, in 1914, was called the "*Comisión Reguladora del Mercado de Henequén*" (Commission for Regulating the Henequen Market), or, for short, the "Reguladora." It was not, however, a great success, for the Reguladora was only an organization buying in competition with the old established agents, and the growers still pursued their own immediate interests in seeking their markets. Coöperation has never been one of the outstanding virtues of the Mexicans, and in the selling of their crops the Yucatecan hacendados have never shown any sign of a break away from the national individualism. The hacendados have always done their business in Merida, the capital and business center of Yucatan. They pass from one sunlit office to another, wailing dismally over the terrible prices the comfortably ensconced buyers offered them and their unfortunate fellows, but seeking and ready at a momentary hint to drive a bargain which would cut their neighbors' throats on the possible chance of a temporary personal profit. The gentlemanly agreement of the

Reguladora was not, under these circumstances, a controlling factor in the henequen market.

This was the situation when, in March, 1915, General Salvador Alvarado, a doughty retainer of President Carranza, "captured" the state of Yucatan with an army of 8,000 men which he had brought from Vera Cruz. Although Mexico has been in revolution since 1911, Yucatan had, till this time, taken little part, accepting new governors with mild surprise but no opposition as one administration succeeded another in Mexico City. Yucatan is a great peninsula far to the east of the Mexican mainland, unconnected by railways, and thirty-six hours' journey by fast steamer across the Gulf of Mexico from Vera Cruz. The Yucatecans have always considered themselves as a people somewhat apart from other Mexicans, and during many of the revolutions previous to Diaz, the peninsula remained aloof and politically independent, re-entering the Mexican confederation only toward the close of the pre-Diaz era.

General Alvarado is a product of northern Mexico. He belongs with the true Carrancista group in Mexican politics, has been a candidate for president of Mexico and has made many trips to the United States as a financier, most recently as an envoy of the de la Huerta government in search of a rehabilitating loan. All this, however, has come since his spectacular experience in Yucatan. In that state he gained the experience, and political record, which made him aspire to the presidency of Mexico, and earned his diploma as revolutionary financier. There, also, he probably first acquired those radical ideas which enabled him to assert, as he did in the Mexican Chamber of Deputies in November of 1920:

"I am a bolshevist, I have always been a bolshevist, and I shall always be a bolshevist."

General Alvarado's first government work was as a custom-house employee, but he joined the Carranza movement early and early rose to the rank of general through the manifestation of a thoroughly forceful personality and a ruthless preoccupation with his own advancement.

Yucatan, in its isolation, in its great wealth, and its easy-going manners, presented General Alvarado with the opportunity of his career. Here were ungathered riches for revolutionary spoils, here was noble opportunity for the uplift of the "submerged 85 per cent," here was waiting easy military glory of conquest with no one to oppose. In going to Yucatan, General Alvarado was, moreover, encumbered by none of the political and business experience which delays the prompt execution of inspired ideas. Nor was he inhibited by any preconception of the needs of the commonwealth or its chief industry, for this was his first visit to his future principality. All he knew or heard was that Yucatan was rich and that its proletariat was "oppressed," largely by wicked foreigners of shocking and predatory manners.

When he arrived in Yucatan, General Alvarado noted with interest the beauty of that gem of Mexican state capitals, Merida, with its sun-clear streets and its beautiful parks and public buildings. He saw the luxurious equipages and homes and visited the great haciendas of henequen. In the meantime, he looked over the documents in the governor's office and the stock of gold in the state treasury. He scowled his disapproval, as was the Carrancista habit, at the foreigners engaged in the henequen business. Then his attention was called to the charter of the Reguladora, the harmless agreement of the hacendados to keep the price of the fiber as high as they could and still not soil their hands with trade.

This charter had courteously made the governor of the state ex-officio head of the Reguladora. Promptly, and without more authority, General Alvarado took charge of the organization. His first act was to force upon the unhappy hacendados, through the authority of their own instrument, a corporation which took their own business utterly out of their own hands and forced them to the acceptance of official dictation without dissent or question.

To the end of organizing his Reguladora in line with modern thought and to thorough efficiency for his own ends, he invited in from Mexico City the one set of brains in the Carranza administration, those of Luis Cabrera, and called in the motley company of self-styled "socialists" who had been drawn to Yucatan by the lurid tales of revolutionary propagandists who had predicted the inevitable uprising of the oppressed proletariat when opportunity should be given them.

This cabinet laid out the Reguladora plan, and two American bankers of New Orleans, Saul Wechsler and Lynn H. Dinkins, organized a syndicate which agreed to finance the cornering of the henequen market up to $10,000,000. There was no socialism in this phase of the plan, for the bankers were to receive a commission of $4 per bale on all henequen marketed, plus the current banking rate of interest for all moneys needed, the loans to be fully secured by mortgages against hemp in storage or in transit.

So far all was well, but here Alvarado met his first difficulty. The henequen growers were not socialistically inclined, nor were they as trusting of his good faith, or so well secured as the American bankers, nor had they so much to gain or so little to lose as the "socialist" advisers of the governor. Many of them refused to be bound by the new rules of the Reguladora, which included, amongst others, a provision that no hemp should be sold to any agent or interest save the Reguladora.

But Alvarado's government called on the hacendados to subscribe to his rules for the Reguladora, and to those who refused it threatened (and gave evidence of the fullness of its intentions to carry out its threats) to fire the fields and throw the offending hacendados and their families into the flames. It organized the Red Guard of Yucatan (called the "Leagues of Resistance"), and spread terrorism throughout the peninsula. It drove out the tiny group of foreigners who for twenty-five years had been engaged in "exploiting" the unfortunate Yucatan proletariat by keeping the capitalistic hacendados from getting too much money out of American farmers. Along with them went hundreds of the hacendados and their families, and also priests and nuns, while the simple Indians who could not take steamers for foreign ports emigrated quietly back into the forests of interior Yucatan.

For Alvarado's henchmen closed the churches, burned their priceless historical records, and outraged nuns and priests. They turned the church buildings into "labor temples" and barracks and storehouses from which later was sold, over the counter, the liquor which had been confiscated in enforcement of "prohibition" in Yucatan. They turned the schools of towns and plantations into centers of propaganda and espionage under imported "teachers" who knew none of the Indian language, and many of whom could not write their own names. They confiscated great haciendas under the elaborately "socialistic" agrarian law, and for those upon whom the iron hand did not fall directly, established a reign of terror in the raids of the "Leagues of Resistance," whose crimes, from night-riding and burglary to rape and murder, the Legislature declared to be "political offenses" in the name of "socialism," and thus outside the jurisdiction of the common courts.

His henchmen, foreigners, Mexicans and Yucatecans, raised up the previously contented "industrial workers," railway men, porters and longshoremen (numbering in all less than 9,000 out of a state population of 300,000), forming them into unions whose increasing wages were overlapped more rapidly than they were raised by the rising costs of the handling of the imported commodities upon which they, like every one else, must live in desert Yucatan. Their wages, and the cost of living, multiplied eight times in the four years, while the wages of the farm workers little more than doubled, and a grievously added burden was placed upon the hacendados who from time immemorial have taken up the loss in increased food prices so that their farm workers may live.

By such means, and with such control, General Alvarado acquired the domination of the industrial life of Yucatan and of henequen production upon which he built up his market corner. In the selling of the product so controlled, he raised the price of raw henequen from 7 cents a pound in New York to more than 19 cents a pound in the same market. So firm was his grip on production and on distribution that he could, and did, withhold stock which was sorely needed in the harvest fields, bringing about, in 1916 (through this means and through the soaring prices which had to be asked for the binder twine which was sold), an investigation by a committee of the United States Senate. This committee, after months of investigation, completely exonerated the American manufacturers from the charge of profiteering, and perhaps for the first time in the history of that august body, placed itself on record as asserting that a foreign government had acted the rôle of an iniquitous trust in creating an artificial shortage and artificially inflated prices for a product vital to the business of America's farms.

In the four years that the Reguladora corner lasted, more than $200,000,000 in advanced prices were taken from American buyers, an average advance of more than 200 per cent. Thus, granting a legitimate doubling of the price of the fiber in keeping with the doubling of the costs of other commodities in this period (1915-1919), the accepted figure of $112,000,000 of direct loot through the Alvarado henequen corner may be taken as literally true. And this was loot that never reached either the cruel hacendados who owned the farms or the workers who furnished the labor for the creation of the product. All this and more went into the bottomless pit of Mexican revolutionary graft.

This henequen corner was, it must be remembered, created in the name of socialism and the salvation of the downtrodden peon. Along with it went a mass of other activities, wherein the funds derived from the sale of henequen at the advancing prices were turned to schemes of ostensible government ownership, socialization and coöperation. Before even the hacendados were given the 4 cents a pound guaranteed them as first payment against the great profits to come from the "corner," the Reguladora funds were invested in the purchase of the state railways, at prices to this day unknown. These funds also financed the organization of the *Compañia de Fomento del Sur-Est* (Development Company of the South-East) and bought nine old Mexican coasting steamers at a cost of $4,000,000 so that the socialists of Yucatan might not be dependent on capitalistic steamship lines. The Reguladora also financed the drilling of oil wells, and built a flock of tanks to contain the oil—which never came out of the ground. It also built a railway, confiscating therefor, "for the common good," one-tenth of all the rails and equipment of the private plantation railways on the henequen farms; in a few months it sold this railway to a favorite for $150,000, a tenth of its cash cost, payable in ten years.

The *Cia. de Fomento del Sur-Est* entered upon the business of relieving the oppressed proletariat from the wicked prices for the necessities of life fixed by capitalistic grocerymen. It bought its own supplies in the United States, transported them in its own steamers, and sold them—for more than the current retail rates! The proletariat did not benefit from any of these schemes, but the government henchmen who bought in the United States, and those who sold in Yucatan, waxed fat and comfortable, although remaining firm and loyal socialists to the end.

All these things were done in the name of socialism, and in that name, also, the power of Reguladora gold was felt even in the heart of the United States, in a heart made sensitive to such machinations by the nervous strain of the war which was already at our throats. Not a little of the money derived from the sale of henequen at prices four and five times normal was used in the conducting of a campaign of propaganda. Mexican and foreign "socialists" were kept in the United States lecturing and writing and publishing magazines and books. These activities were radical and, in part at least, I. W. W., in general character but they were devoted also to spreading the fame of the Alvarado brand of socialization of industry in Yucatan and to the dissemination of anti-American ideas under the guise of socialism.

It was glory and it was madness to strike thus at the heart of the "Colossus of the North" as the anti-foreign Mexican orators like to call the United States, and at the very same time at the "Colossus of Mammon," as the wilder socialists referred to us in Yucatan. Carranza had tried the former form of baiting, but the combination of the two was an orgy of glory reserved for the satellites of Alvarado. Never was anything quite so daring and quite so magnificent ever done by a Mexican revolutionist before, and not even Carranza dared do more.

So glory and madness traveled together, but meanwhile, out in the henequen fields and in the Indian villages, Yucatan toiled on. The simple natives could not quite appreciate the "socialists" and literally fled in terror before some of their manifestations, so that in that day, and in this as well, they tell you with eager friendship to "beware of these terrible socialists." To them, "socialist" is a name associated with things that are, to their simple minds, quite unsocial.

Alvarado, in his "conquest" of Yucatan, had frankly spread terror throughout the peninsula. Opposed, on his triumphal march to Merida, by a small "home guard" of upper and middle class youths, he had captured and shot scores of them in cold blood, as "traitors," and pursued his way. He had, as I have noted, closed and sacked the churches, remarking that "As the revolution advances, God recedes." Then, on one of the main boulevards of Merida, he had allowed the dead bodies of two who had offended him to swing from sunrise to sunset from a limb of an oak tree, so that thereafter the simple words, "Remember the oak tree," were sufficient to bring the stoutest-hearted conservative to terms.

But for all that, General Alvarado protested unfailing friendship for the peons and the Indians, grieved somewhat by their distrust of him, but pronouncing his devotion to their welfare in no measured terms. In his carrying out of his "socialistic" policies, he did not, however, consult their wishes or even their possibilities of development. His one panacea for the ills of the Indians was "land," and land he and his imported advisers were determined to give them, no matter whether they wanted it or not. Never did the ideals of socialism, beautiful in themselves, have an uglier distortion.

"Land distribution" is, as I have said, the crux of the protestations of all Mexican revolutionists. Upon the alleged land hunger of the Indians the revolutionists have based most of their appeals for foreign sympathy. The actual facts of the labor situation, in Mexico and especially in Yucatan, are therefore worth brief description in this connection. The so-called "peonage system" of Mexico goes back historically to pre-Spanish times. It is based on the psychological difficulty of obtaining continuous labor. Continuous labor being vital to such an industry as henequen growing, there flourished in Yucatan, previous to 1914, a system of indebtedness which was practically slavery. Laborers on the plantations were allowed to get into debt in order that they might be held on the plantations on the pretext of working out the advances which were made from time to time by the hacendados. These debts averaged about 200 pesos ($100) a man, and it is undoubtedly true that the system was the origin of wicked abuses, a plantation store credit system being devised to keep the peons always in debt, and workers being sold by the head for their debts. Confinement in barbed wire enclosures was common in some sections, and altogether the picture of the Yucatan situation especially was a very unlovely one.

But the system of debt advances was really effectively abolished under Madero, two full years before Carranza and Alvarado entered upon the scene, and it is worth noting that the hacendados, many of whom had fortunes tied up in peon debts, found themselves far happier to be free from the system than were the peons. It is indeed questionable whether the peonage system, as such (and where it was not abused), was entirely distasteful to the Indians who were its victims. Lacking any ability to save, the abolition of the system of debt advances wrenched from their grasp the only possible form of enjoying the fruits of their labor outside their usual hand-to-mouth existence. Under the old systems they were able to have some of the good things of life by getting an advance in money, which they spent gayly, careless of the future, and then proceeded to work out the debt in the months or years which followed. Basically, the system had its redeeming features, when considered from the viewpoint of Indian psychology, even though the abuses were such that its abolition was inevitable.

Linked up with the peonage system was the land distribution question, far too complicated for its origins to be gone into here.[6] In Yucatan, the most heavily populated section is not the most fertile. Henequen is not grown in the forests back from the sandy seacoast where prehistoric civilization left the great ruins of a rich and glorious empire, but on the seacoast itself. This virtual desert, extending in some places twenty-five miles back from the coast, is the land which is adapted to the growing of henequen, for a slow maturing of the plant is vital to the creation of those long, strong fibers which constitute the valuable portion of the leaves.

This so-called desert land is sometimes capable, when first cleared of brush, of one or even two croppings of corn. Then it must lie fallow for many years before another food crop can be raised. The native Indian, therefore, has little or no use for a small plot, or indeed for the ownership of any plot of ground, unless he can crop it once or twice and then sell it to a henequen planter, while the Indian seeks other corn-lands elsewhere. If the government hampers him in moving about, he prefers not to try to live as an independent farmer, but to work on a plantation where he can get regular pay for cutting henequen leaves, and also can cultivate a little corn-plot lent him by the hacendado and renewed each year.

Now the Indian, despite the fortunes which have been made by the hacendados in the henequen business, has no interest at all in becoming a henequen grower. He knows from experience that the value of the leaves he himself produces are little more than what he would be paid on an hacienda for cutting the hacendado's own leaves, and he knows that he has not the capital or the initiative to go into hemp production himself. The result was that some years ago, when the communal land was first distributed to the Indians, it was cropped once or twice and then sold to the nearest hacendado to become henequen plots.

Sometimes indeed, the communal land was so worthless for corn that the hacendados were allowed to take it over without payment or protest and to plant it to henequen. This loss, from the Indian viewpoint, was far from an unmixed evil, for the natives of the commune profited in the gaining of an opportunity for assured livelihood close by their homes—difficult enough except on the henequen farms, in the desert sections of Yucatan.

Henequen production is far more of an industry than it is a farming project. Primarily, it requires from the planting of the shoots until the first leaves are ready for cutting, eight years of continual and expensive care, for the fields must be kept clear of brush and weeds, the plants tended and those which die replaced with regularity. After eight years of continuous outlay, the leaves are cut, brought into a great industrial plant where machinery and many workers are required to remove the pulp, to dry the hemp fiber on racks under the sun, to pack it into 400-pound bales in hydraulic presses, and to ship it to the distant American market. The agricultural end of the henequen business is but a small item in its process, and no individual farmer, even if he has moderate capital, can prosper on it.

The land distribution planned by Alvarado was to be made from the great henequen haciendas, and some of the oratory defending the confiscation of those haciendas pointed out the fact that this very land had been stolen from the Indian communes in years gone by and was now being returned to the original Indian owners. That was interesting to the pitying audiences of the Alvarado propagandists in the United States, but it was of not the slightest interest to the Indians of Yucatan. They had once owned that land, and had or had not cropped it in corn once or twice. They knew quite well it was hardly worth the trouble and the expense in taxes it would be for them to own it again, especially as they saw the hacendados being skillfully put out of business and knew that with their disappearance went the only market in which Indians could sell the land after they got it, or the henequen leaves if they raised them.

Thus it came about that despite the apparent incongruity of the fact, the Indians of Yucatan paid almost no attention to Alvarado's land distribution plans, listening to the alluring official announcements with stolid indifference. They attended the festivals which accompanied the distribution, but they took up no land grants.

There were indeed, many Indians who actually took flight into the interior of the state as a result of the efforts to force land upon them. The Mexican Indian, of whatever tribe, in reality desires deeply but one thing—to be left alone to pursue his half-savage life in his own way, an aboriginal ambition which should not be difficult to understand by those who know anything of the North American Indian of the United States. Socialism, like the responsibilities of land ownership, is beyond his ken and he literally ran away from the offers of either in Yucatan.

Some Indians, of course, remained, along with a great number of the mixed-blood "slaves" who had been imported from the Mexican mainland into the state during the boom period of the henequen business. These were thoroughly "unionized" in the Mexican sense. That is, they were forced to pay their poor little three pesos for a big red card which proclaimed their membership in some union or other, were promised all that the human heart could desire—and were allowed to subsist as long as possible upon the promises. The unions were used to the double end of ruining the capitalistic landlords and reducing the output of henequen so that the price would go higher.

On the plantations where these "unionized" workmen remained, the old task system, by which each man cut from 2,500 to 3,000 leaves a day, was abandoned for a regular "eight-hour day" in which the workmen did as little as they cared to do, and worked, not under instructions, but wherever they chose to work. As a result the cutting of leaves was reduced fully one-half, and the plants near the roads were overcut while those deep in the fields were allowed to blossom and go to seed. Both processes killed the henequen, which has to be cut regularly and skillfully in order to prolong its life of usefulness. For miles the great pole-like blossoms marked the henequen fields like a forest, and thousands of productive acres went to ruin. Thus Nature's inevitable process of flowering and decay marked, itself, man's crass flinging back of her riches into the dust from which those riches had come in the long slow years of his care of her.

Meanwhile, other forces had been at work, some building the pyramid of mad ideas and madder methods, others undermining the pyramid's foundations upon the rocks of the conservative past or disintegrating its mortar of imitation socialistic idealism. Of these forces, the greatest was the financial cycle of paper money, "short" drafts and towering mortgages against increasing stocks of unsold henequen.

By 1915, when Alvarado arrived in Yucatan, the system of paper money which Carranza used to finance his revolution had already engulfed Mexico. Carranza had recently issued his famous dictum that if Gresham's law (one of the fundamental laws of economics, which holds that bad money, in any quantity, inevitably drives out good money) was interfering with the circulation of the Carranza paper, Gresham's law should forthwith be repealed by executive decree. Billions of Carranza paper had been printed, and it was already the circulating medium in Yucatan; gold and bank bills were in hiding. Alvarado decided that the time was ripe for a currency of his own, and issued, before he had been long in the state, the Reguladora paper money, ostensibly guaranteed by hemp in storage in Yucatan and in the United States. By decree, this money had to be received at the old value of the silver peso, two for one American dollar.

It was a beautiful idea, except for economic law. The bayonets of Alvarado's soldiers helped keep up values for a while, but slowly the theory that power can achieve anything the "proletariat" wants was blasted by fact. Alvarado had promised to redeem his Reguladora paper in gold or in New York exchange, but he did not bother to back up his promises by a limitation of the currency to the amount he could redeem, so that at one time he had $34,000,000 in paper in circulation, against henequen stores of half the value, stores which he could not liquidate. The currency's value dropped, cent by cent, then by groups of cents, and finally it was almost waste paper, like that of Carranza. There was not enough henequen in New

York, nor enough gold in Yucatan, to redeem the paper, and the political nostrum for the economic ill of bad paper currency failed.

The failure was colossal enough, in any case, without the financial complication of the currency. Alvarado had closed the ports to all hemp from the interior that was not consigned to the Reguladora. That beneficent monopoly allowed no shipments by rail, and before he got through Alvarado had to close the roads with soldiers, so that no carts could reach the port. Meanwhile, he had been boosting the price, deliberately and virtually by decree, until, as I have said, it reached more than 19 cents, as against less than 7 cents a pound which had been its price before the Reguladora took charge of the market.

This raising of the price cut off a large portion of the market,—and that had not been anticipated. Virtually all consumption of henequen except for binder twine ceased. At 19 cents Manila hemp could compete—and it is far better hemp. At 19 cents jute cord can compete, and jute cord is soft and pleasant to handle, and where previously henequen cord had been used for big bundles of newspapers and magazines and mail, jute was substituted—and now the men who handle the bundles of newspapers and magazines and mail refuse to go back to the rasping henequen cord which cuts their hands so uncomfortably.

The consumption of henequen was actually reduced to half by this deliberate destruction of its market. In spite of the new low prices to-day, this condition in the general fiber market combines with the cutting off of the Russian and some of the other European demand to reduce the world consumption of the Yucatan fiber to about 70 per cent of what it was prior to 1914. All this loss the Reguladora had to take up, in addition to the stores which it laid aside to push up the price. Economic law was at work, and all the contentious statements that the price was going up only in proportion to the rising costs the world over was answered by the fact that henequen was driven out of the general fiber market by other hemps which had increased in price, to be sure, but had never approached the geometrical progression which henequen assumed under the lordly sway of Alvarado's corner.

When all is said and done, however, it was Mother Nature and Gresham's law which finally broke the corner. Corners in the products of Nature have a way of piling up unexpected responsibilities and finally loosing unexpected forces which swamp the unwary juggler. So it was in Yucatan. With about a year's supply of fiber in storage in the United States and Mexico, more than half of it mortgaged to American bankers, and with about $10,000,000 in Reguladora currency in circulation with nothing but photographs of gold stores to guarantee it, Alvarado's henequen corner went the way of all the corners of history. That was in the spring of 1920 when, after a year of price fluctuation, Nature and the eternal laws of economics began gently wafting the prices downward until they reached the lowest level in fifteen years. Then it was that the banking syndicate, which had loaned money against henequen shipments, foreclosed on 250,000 bales in storage in New York, marking the final chapter in the story of Alvarado's Reguladora experiment.

When the smash came, there was an Association of Henequen Growers which had been begging in Yucatan and in the Supreme Court of Mexico for a chance to take back their business. As the financial difficulties and the financial needs of Alvarado's henchmen increased, the Reguladora had all but given up paying any money to the haciendas where the henequen was produced. The mule that lived on sawdust up to the day he died is a fable of ancient times, but even under such loudly acclaimed "socialism" as that of Yucatan something has to be paid for a product which is produced and exported. The growers had all but reached the end of their resources, and Alvarado offered them only paper money, which he would or could not change into gold drafts. So just before the crash, to satisfy the clamor, Alvarado took his way to Mexico City and royally presented the Reguladora to the Association of the Producers of Henequen.

The hacendados had hardly had time to look over the ruins when those financial interests which had loaned money on hemp that was to sell around 20 cents a pound foreclosed on those 250,000 bales in New York and New Orleans, placing thereon a value of 5 cents a pound. Alvarado was safe in Mexico City preparing to visit New York in an effort to get a loan of a few hundred millions for the government of Carranza. The hacendados held the sack, and watching the sack was a group of financiers, including the Equitable Trust Company of New York, the Royal Bank of Canada and the Interstate Trust Company of New Orleans, the latter the Dinkins concern through which most of the loans on the henequen had been placed.

Down in Yucatan the hacendados had their farms back, the Indians were returning at night to look things over and see whether the "socialists" had retired far enough for them to return in safety to their comfortable "slavery"—but nobody had any money. When Alvarado left, the hacendados had inherited the Reguladora offices, and had opened its money vaults. These vaults, photographs of whose gold stocks had been circulated by Alvarado to sustain his paper currency, were quite empty. The haciendas were in terrible condition, and there was no way of getting funds with which to rebuild and replant them. The only hope was for capital from outside—Alvarado's "socialism" had passed on its way. Of the possible sources of rescue, the chief was in the group of unhappy banks in New York, New Orleans and Montreal, which were already in the henequen business with their 250,000 bales of foreclosed stock. The second hope was the International Harvester Company, which needs henequen in its business. The hacendados chose the banks, and the Equitable Trust Company, the Royal Bank of Canada, the Interstate Trust Co., and the Comisión Reguladora (which still existed in name if not in spirit) formed a company, and taking the four initials, called themselves the Eric Corporation.

There was much rejoicing in Yucatan, for the Eric was going to lend a few more paltry American and Canadian millions and reëstablish the great state industry. The Reguladora (now consisting of the hacendados) turned in some 300,000 more bales of hemp that were stored at Progreso, the Yucatan port, as their part of the capital stock of the Eric, and the hacendados went back to work.

Now one of the peculiar things about "economic ruin" is that it seldom ruins a business—individuals are the only victims. Yucatan was devastated, many thousands of acres put on the non-productive list. There was no money to pay labor or to finance the crops, but the henequen business went on. To all intents and purposes about all that had happened was the elimination of most of the surplus planting which there would have been if all had gone along properly and there had been no Alvarado to corner and destroy the market. Henequen kept on growing on the haciendas and, despite increased costs of handling, it continued to move to market.

Don Avelino Montes, a Spaniard who had been the chief buyer of the International Harvester Company, returned from his exile in Cuba and resumed buying. Don Arturo Pierce, the honorary British vice-consul who did the buying for the Plymouth Cordage Company, abandoned consuling and returned to the henequen trade. The price of Yucatan hemp kept slumping, but to the surprise of the Eric people, the demand was supplied with new hemp, and the Eric's stocks of old hemp diminished but slightly. The money to rehabilitate the Yucatan haciendas was not forthcoming. The old hemp stock had to be sold first, and the wretched hacendados refused to coöperate and let the Eric unload.

Henequen deteriorates, and also it requires insurance, as the many fires in Progreso and New Orleans at the time testified. The cost of holding the half million bales of henequen of the Eric is about $2,500,000 a year, and the price at which it was bought in, plus insurance, represents a cost of about 8 cents a pound. The price of hemp had been stabilized at that very figure by Señores Montes and Pierce, with some outside assistance from New York brokers, but the sales were made in Yucatan, of new hemp. So the Eric, in righteous anger, cut the price from 8 cents to 7, and then to 6. The price of new hemp also fell, and the hacendados, partners in the Eric, wailed at the evil which was being done them. However, they continued to sell the new crop at the new price, to the Harvester and the Plymouth and Henry Peabody & Co., and Hanson and Orth, while the gradually deteriorating stocks of the Eric went begging. The price was finally cut to 5 cents, by the Eric. Yucatan has met this price, too, with new hemp, and because it is still possible to make money out of henequen with the price at 4 cents in New York, it seems likely that Yucatan will continue to grow henequen, and to sell it. Meanwhile, however, the business doctors of the Obregon administration in Mexico City at one time succumbed to the pressure of the unhappy hacendados and even agreed to try the "Reguladora" experiment all over again, with the central government buying 60 per cent of the henequen crop at 6 cents a pound, and again "controlling" the market, a step in the spiral of destruction which had but a brief life and little significance. For the story of Yucatan is written and the state and its great industry are to-day being ground between the wheels of the "capitalism" which the beautiful theories of Yucatan's "socialistic" autocrats sought to destroy.

This is the outcome of Yucatan's experiments in Alvarado's brand of so-called socialism. The price of the fiber is back to less than it was before the inflation began, the production has been cut from 1,000,000 bales in 1914 to less than 700,000 in 1919, a decline of 30 per cent, while, taking the potential production from the plantings up to 1914, the present production is about half of what it would have been if Alvarado had never come to Yucatan. The haciendas are back in the hands of their original owners, the market is in the hands of foreign capital, and foreign capital is fighting over the spoils with what seems to the Yucatecans utter and cruel disregard of the amenities of gentlemen. The $112,000,000 squeezed from American farmers and the other untold millions taken from Yucatan by loot, by false prices in "coöperative stores," by freight rates on the graft-owned railways, and all the other means used by Alvarado's retainers, have gone to the enrichment of his group and to the upkeeping of the Carranza government. No noticeable part of it has remained in Yucatan, and save for increased wages all around (and the world has surely learned that this is not prosperity) no possible profit has remained. The spiral cycle is complete, and none has gained, not even the predatory capitalists, who are unhappily cutting each other's throats in an effort to solve the problems into which they were swept by the machinations of Alvarado and his henchmen.

To-day Yucatan is not free from the domination of the "socialists," but that domination is political, marked by those outrages which have come to be merely a part of politics in Mexico. Elections are held from time to time, elections wherein two parties of socialists alone confronted each other. The battle is bitter, as battles are when brothers are the contestants. There is still killing and loot, and women and children suffer death and worse in the solution of such glowing political questions as whether, we might say, the flag of Yucatan should be all red or merely red with a black bar across it—its problems are daily forgotten, for the real issue is only to find out who should have the next hand at the graft. Socialistic, to be sure, because all Mexican manifestations to-day are masquerading under the name of socialism, but quite as little in tune with true socialistic ideals as a battle between two factions in Tammany Hall over the control of New York politics would be socialism.

FOOTNOTES

[6] Both peonage and the Mexican systems of land distribution are discussed at some length in *The People of Mexico*.

CHAPTER VIII
THE ROMANCE OF MEXICAN OIL

When you cross the Mexican border at Laredo, oil enters your consciousness—and your clothes. It is everywhere, the thick, odorous *chapapote* which furnishes the fuel for Mexico's locomotives, the energy for every Mexican industry which has no water power, the pavements for her streets, and, I am still convinced, the heavy lubricant with which the sandal-clad brakeman of our train eased an incidental hot-box. In Tampico, whence comes all the oil of Mexico, the heavy, black "crude" is even more ubiquitous. It "tars" your shoes when you walk abroad; it decorates your clothes when you ride in anybody's motor car or motor boat; it oozes between your toes and sticks in your hair when you bathe at the beach.

But the physical presence of oil is as a whiff from the dead well at Dos Bocas compared to its spiritual domination in all Mexican affairs. Oil is the greatest—I had almost said the only—wealth of Mexico to-day, its possession the issue of one of the mighty diplomatic battles of recent times, while the taxes and graft of it have fed the wellsprings of ten years of devastating revolutions.

Far and away and by many fold, oil is the largest single item of export of Mexico, and the varied needs of the oil industry and of the beneficiaries of that industry dominate the imports as well. To Tampico go shiploads of steel, machinery and supplies, and trainloads of soap and shoes; the factors which build civilization go chiefly and all but alone, in Mexico, to the oil fields.

Oil dominates the political life of the country not because oil companies or oil millionaires seek to control the Mexican government but because the vast unbelievable wealth which is pouring into the coffers of that government in taxes and in tribute makes revolution a game the stakes of which eclipse any sum or any potentiality of wealth or power which has ever been known in Mexico.

Oil is the inspiration for the "nationalization" policies which, forged by foreign radicals and given edge by Mexican cupidity, the Carrancistas wrote into their Constitution of 1917. This policy of nationalization, the decrees, the laws, the taxation and the graft which have come in its train, have brought into the field of diplomatic controversy the whole problem of the right of a government to enforce radical, socialistic or, if you will, bolshevik policies against foreign interests which may have entered a country and developed it under older, more conservative ideals and systems of government.

For the oil industry of Mexico is overwhelmingly a foreign enterprise. American and British and Dutch are the flags which should fly from the oil derricks, for neither Mexico nor Mexicans have had a hand worth the naming in the opening of the nation's richest treasure-house. The search for oil in Mexico has taken on the nature of a race, a battle, between British and American oil interests, a battle not without its tremendous significance in the world oil situation. But behind this struggle, which is still and, we may hope, will remain a friendly one, loom controversies which are vaster than Mexico or England or America, problems on whose solution the very future of our civilization depends.

For the real battle in Mexico is not between the two great Anglo-Saxon powers, but between the powers of light and the powers of darkness. In Mexico's oil fields to-day is being settled the question of whether enterprise shall have the right to bring the riches of the earth to the aid of humanity, of whether industrial power belongs to the backward people who by accident find that power in their inept hands, or to those who can develop and raise it up to the service of mankind. Upon the issue in Mexico depends not only the usefulness of all the petroleum resources of that country, but the future development of oil in Colombia, Venezuela, all South America, all Asia, all Africa. And the future of oil development in those lands is the future of the world's oil supply, for there, alone, remain stores sufficient to meet the multiplying needs of the world.

The solution of this question is vastly complicated. Within the oil situation itself are many problems such as those just noted. Bearing upon it is the tangle of cross-purposes, indirections and varying psychologies. That solution is made all but impossible by the conditions of Mexico to-day, by the flabby weakness of the rulers of the Mexican people, by their blindness and selfishness. It has been jammed, time and again, by the failure of the oil companies and their representatives to assert their rights with a skill equal to that of the Mexicans in casting up mountains of controversy out of mole hills of technicality.

But the story of Mexican oil is not all ugly calling of names, not all mere hopeless tangle. The history of its discovery and development is rich with color. The romance of an oil field, like the romance of a gold camp, is always a thrilling tale. But the story of Tampico has this other element, for it is indeed the great romance of our race, the tale of the white man round the world, the building of gigantic enterprises, the harnessing of unknown forces, neglected for centuries by apathetic natives, unlocked by the vision and the enterprise of the Anglo-Saxon.

Oil began with Tampico, but the story of Tampico antedates oil. It goes back to the late 80's, when one of the great railway builders of America's youth left Kansas for Mexico. A. A. Robinson, who surveyed and built the Santa Fe Railroad from the Kansas prairies to the Pacific Ocean, who swung the track of the Denver and Rio Grande Railroad above the rapids of the Royal Gorge, was also one of the great builders of modern Mexico. Leaving the Santa Fe in 1889, he became president of the Mexican Central and built almost the whole of this first standard gauge line in the country, its branches and tributaries toward the rich granary of Mexico about Guadalajara in the west, to the mines of Pachuca in the mountains and to Tampico on the Gulf of Mexico.

Tampico, a wretched, fever-ridden village beside a beautiful river, was no port in those days. The railroad which brought Mr. Robinson to Tampico brought also the engineers who built the great jetties which cleared the bar and opened Tampico to the world, carried the ores of Pachuca to their markets and began the conscious development of what is now the busiest seaport of Mexico. The railroad company built and paid for the jetties, and under Mr. Robinson a short-line to Mexico City was surveyed and construction was begun, to be halted, in 1908, by the government merger of the lines.

All this seems to lead far away from oil, but it was in 1900, two years before the jetties were completed, that Mr. Robinson invited Edward L. Doheny and his partner, the late Charles A. Canfield, to Tampico to develop oil wells. Doheny, who had made himself famous and unpopular by discovering petroleum in the middle of Los Angeles, came to examine the seepages of which Robinson had told him in the hope that he might find an oil to help the Mexican Central solve its fuel problems, for the coal of Mexico is scarce and poor, and all the fuel for the railways had to be imported.

Mr. Robinson agreed to buy the oil for fuel if Mr. Doheny developed it, and it was this encouragement, this faith of two great believers in Mexico, which brought about the discovery and the later development of Mexican oil. The board of directors for the Mexican Central later repudiated the Robinson contract, but the development of the Mexican oil fields had been begun, and it has never stopped from that day to this.

It was in 1905 that I first visited Tampico. I was the guest of Mr. Robinson, and as we looked out, one day, over the marshes along the river which runs past Tampico to the sea, six miles away, he told me of his dreams for his port, of the day when not only the Tampico side of the river, but the barren jungle on the other bank would be lined with wharves and great steamers, greater than any of the coasters and tramps that to the number of half a dozen a month were then carrying coal and ore and, amusingly enough as we look back on it now, crude oil from Pennsylvania for use in Tampico's one industrial establishment, the Waters-Pierce Refinery.

I visited Tampico twice again, the last time in 1908. And then this year! It was as if the dream of the builder of the port had come true since the setting of yesterday's sun. To-day the river is lined, from its mouth all the six miles to Tampico and above, with wharves and warehouses and hundreds of great tanks of oil, and throughout all this length are ships, tankers and cargo boats, while on the hills above are refineries and modern towns, and at night the lights are like those of great cities. The dream, indeed, of a builder of civilization, of civilized Mexico, has apparently come true.

A. A. Robinson is gone, laid away with his honors and his vision these four years. But still there is that other American, who twenty years ago rode off into the jungles of the coastal plain, saw with his own eyes the thick, slimy puddles of asphalt at Ebano, and there drilled his first wells. Years later, after his railway contracts were abrogated, seeking lighter, better oils, Mr. Doheny went, with the frontiersman's unquenchable optimism, nearly a hundred miles farther into the jungle till he heard the unforgettable baby murmur and saw the unforgettable bubbling spring of viscous black oil of the great seepages of Cerro Azul, and there located what was to become the greatest oil well in the history of the world, the Cerro Azul No. 4.

Oil is the most fascinating of all the treasures of earth. No geologist has ever approached the solution of either its source or the contours or formations within which it lies. An oil spring such as that wonderful bubbling pool at Cerro Azul may mean the presence of a great reservoir of oil directly beneath or it may mean that the oil has come a dozen or fifty or a hundred miles along a crack in the mother-rock. Experience, faith, intuition, these determine the location of a well. It was these factors that Doheny brought with him to Mexico, for the fields which he finally drilled and proved had been rejected by many geologists before he came and after.

At Ebano, a way-station on the Mexican Central a few miles inland from Tampico this pioneer of the Mexican oil fields found his oil and developed it, and his success brought hundreds of other prospectors to Ebano in 1900-1902. But Ebano oil is heavy with asphalt, and it was dangerous to handle in the crude burners of the time because its fumes ignite at low temperatures. Thus, although it is rich in lubricating oils, it was not the petroleum which the world wanted in that day. With his contract with the Mexican Central abrogated, virtually without a market excepting for asphalt paving in Mexican cities, Doheny turned southward in search of lighter oils.

His trips into the swamps and forests of the *huasteca* or coastal plain led him to the great seepages at Cerro Azul, sixty miles below Ebano. It also took him to Juan Casiano where he located his first wells and in 1908 opened the first of the great producing pools of the Tuxpam district. Drilling and exploration went hand in hand and not only Doheny but the British interests of Sir Weetman Pearson (now Lord Cowdray) and other American companies began to make this field famous.

Since that time the story of the Tampico oil fields has been the story of the Americans and other foreigners who followed them. No Mexican name and no Mexican interest are connected with the vast development which has come. Yet so vast is the busy zone of production, so tremendous and so varied the forces and elements working there, that one feels something false in this appearance of preponderance of individuals and of foreigners in the epochal industry of Mexico. When, however, one glimpses the long diplomatic struggle, the legal tangle, the endless problems which make the Mexican oil question so complicated, one finds that in every phase there are always only these foreigners on the one side and the predatory, scheming Mexican revolutionary leaders on the other. Never is there a Mexican on the production side, never a foreigner on the side of the elements which retard production.

It was Mr. Robinson who opened up Mexican oil, and it was Doheny and other early foreigners who first dared drill, and the foreigners alone who in the years past have dared to put millions into pipe lines, storage tanks and wonderful fleets of oil-carrying ships. Only they dared or would dare to go into the sleepy villages of the Vera Cruz plains and pay fifty cents a day to peons who had lived for generations on less than a quarter as much. Only the foreigners dared give their labor a decent wage, dared teach their men to be worth more and more until to-day they pay the commonest peon the equivalent of two American dollars a day. Only these foreigners dared believe in Mexico, dared insist on the good faith of all her faithless governments, dared to go on with their work when all else in Mexico stagnates and cringes before the continuing revolutions.

And on the other hand are the Mexicans who govern the land, making it their chief business to bait and loudly curse these same foreigners. The name of the foreign oil men is anathema in Mexico to-day, and the busiest game of any Mexican official is the oratorical denouncing of the sponsors of the industry. But, we cannot forget, these Mexicans have not and do not turn a finger to the replacing of great foreign activity by any constructive form of Mexican enterprise.

At basis the difficulties of the oil companies and the Mexican governments are psychological—and an understanding of those psychological bases is the rarest flower in the intellectual nosegay of most of those who discuss either Mexico or oil. First of all is the companies' belligerent insistence on the principles of vested rights as the first and only basis for the oil discussion—naturally distasteful to those whose single idea is to upset those rights. Another psychological element is that the foreigners' very respect for law and the continuity of government and their insistence that Mexico live up to their own ideals is in the first place quite beyond the conception of the Mexicans in power to-day and in the second place such an attitude is inevitably maddening to the weaker brother whom it seeks to benefit. Because the foreigners believe in Mexico, the Mexicans will not believe in the foreigners.

Another disturbing factor is the very success of the oil companies and of the foreigners whom they employ. I have told, above, something of the picture of the Tampico that was and of the Tampico that is. It has changed in yet other ways, and most of all in the makeup of her population.

In 1908 there were perhaps two score Americans and English in the town, and the chief industry of the place was—tarpon fishing! To-day there are 8,000 Americans and a thousand British and Dutch, and the swaggering, free-money, noisy, busy atmosphere of the frontier, of the oil fields, of the white man on his bully-ragging, destructive, inconsequential "education" of the dark brother round the world, permeates the place. Its influence is not academic, but somehow one feels that Tampico is a monument to the genius and faith of the Americans who made it great. The restless power is there, the restless making over of the world that it may be a better place for the white youth of the future to stamp about in, for the dark brothers to build their new homes in.

Yet strangely enough, if you will, it is to my mind largely because of this same energy, the achievement which this spirit indicates and predicates, that the difficulties of the foreign oil companies in Mexico have been the sort they are. Their persecution has sprung from the realization of the Mexicans that these Americans, these English, these Dutch, are doing in Mexico and for Mexico what Mexicans can not, dare not, do. The Mexicans from generals to peons, are frantic, baffled, rabid, at the wretched Gringoes who dare to pour their millions out to drill wells, to build pipe lines and terminals and ships, to take and to convert this black and liquid gold from the soil of Mexico.

Of the hundreds of wells drilled in the Tampico-Tuxpam fields, some of them the veriest "wildcats" on the flimsiest of chances, hundreds of them as sure as opening a bank vault, only a half dozen, and none a "wildcat," have been drilled by Mexicans as individuals or in corporations, and not a single ship, not a single storage tank, not a mile of pipe line, is Mexican. Were the Mexican government to take over the administration of the oil fields to-day, drilling would cease utterly, to-morrow development would stop and when, a year hence, it became vital to open more wells, the event would be marked by government ceremonies and stifling graft.

Every one who knows Mexico knows that this is the truth. The Mexicans themselves know it, and from the Tampico policeman who howls in outraged anger when an American motorist refuses to be disturbed by official anathemas, up to the presidential secretaries who devise complicated and childish schemes to force the oil companies into recognizing the dignity of Mexican sovereignty, the whole attitude toward the oil business has been fraught with effort to maintain that hazy halo of the weakling, delicate "sensitiveness," national pride, *amour propre*.

When I left New York to study Mexican problems for the present writing, I was convinced that the full facts of the case, on both sides, were to be found in the United States; Washington was indeed the battle ground of lawyers and diplomats. Not until I reached Tampico, however, not until I went out to the oil fields, did I realize that the real problem is not the question of diplomatic controversy or commercial adjustment. There, on the long roads, where but one *peon* of all the thousands whom we passed, took off his hat to the white *patrones*, as every one would have done twelve years ago, I found the touchstone. I knew then why reason will not prevail, why justice is non-existent, why no white man has yet been able to feel firm ground beneath his feet in the discussion of the oil problems. These problems have had their rights and wrongs, as we shall see, but I think that the great difficulty we at home have had in believing that our own people could be right has been our inability to conceive how, being right, the Mexicans could be so hostile to them.

This, I think, is the point of departure in our misunderstanding of the Mexican situation, especially as it applies to oil. Mexican jealousy and Mexican realization of the weakness of the national psychology in great enterprise have set Mexico frantic with the success, the triumph, the apparent imperturbability of the great foreign oil companies. This alone has made their hostility to the American drillers, linemen and engineers who night and day, month after month through the years of the war, kept the lines open, the oil flowing. Unarmed, and slaughtered by the score from ambush, grim, unkempt, often happily drunk in town, these frontiersmen added their bit to the fire, to be sure. But note this—it was not the white man's rough assertion of superiority or the companies' "tactless insistence," but the Mexican's conception of his own inferiority, personal, commercial, political, which lit the flame and kept it burning.

The world has entered upon a new industrial era, the age of petroleum. The commercial struggle is to-day not the war for markets, but the race for oil lands. And of all the petroleum fields known to exist, those in Mexico are the greatest in actual production, the greatest in potential extent, and the most favorably situated for distribution—all vivified by the greatest individual oil wells in the records of the world.

The story of the development of that oil field is linked with the history of Mexico, inexorably, inevitably a part of it, influencing it, all but dominating it.

The first oil well in Mexico was brought in in 1900; production began on a commercial scale in 1903; about 1904 a British company secured its first "concession" for oil drilling; in 1905 the status of petroleum as belonging to the owner of the surface land was definitely settled, and development began on a large scale; in 1912 the Madero government established, over the mild protests of the producing companies, the principle of special taxation on the oil business; in 1914 President Huerta extracted 200,000 Mexican pesos from an American oil representative in Mexico City, and the oil company, under advice of the Department of State, repudiated his draft and paid the money to Carranza; in 1914 the principle of "shaking down" the oil companies was originated by Candido Aguilar (later son-in-law of Carranza), who made a mild $10,000 collection; in 1915 Manuel Pelaez made his first call for tribute, some $1,500, under the exchange conditions of the day, which the companies paid with the advice of the American State Department and the American Ambassador, a precedent which later netted Pelaez a regular $30,000 a month; in 1915 Carranza began to devote the brains of his finance minister, Luis Cabrera, to devising oil taxes, with the result that to-day the foreign oil companies pay a total of nearly $4,000,000 a month, derived from export taxes on the product, stamp taxes on their business, occupation taxes on their offices, harbor taxes on their ships, customs duties on their supplies, etc.; in 1916 Carranza issued the decree requiring foreigners who did business in Mexico to renounce their rights of recourse to their home government; in 1917 came the new Mexican constitution declaring all petroleum in the subsoil the property of the nation; in 1919 the drilling of new wells was stopped unless the companies agreed to accept this principle of nationalization; in 1919 the second of the big oil pools went to salt water and the need of new drilling to keep up the supply of oil (and the Mexican taxes) became imperative; in January, 1920, temporary drilling permits were issued by Carranza; in May, 1920, Carranza was overthrown and murdered in the revolution of Obregon, said to have been financed by certain oil interests; in 1921 Obregon doubled the oil taxes, bringing about a shutdown, temporary but salutary; in 1921 drilling is going on, however, and the shipment of oil continues.

While drilling is going on in small sections in spite of obstacles, the full development of the petroleum fields of Mexico waits on the final decision of the confiscatory provisions of Carranza, whose dead hand still guides the policies of his successors along the road of anti-foreignism. In 1921, then, the oil companies are still uncertain of their status, still the objects of astonishing taxation, still subject to government annoyance and graft, still buying, in taxes and annoyances, the "privilege" of working their properties.

The plants of the foreign companies are probably the greatest installation in any single oil field in the world. The investment in pipe lines, pumping stations, storage tanks, refineries, terminals and ships represents close on $750,000,000; the length of the 161 pipe lines (practically all of them eight or ten inches in diameter) totals nearly 1,000 miles, while nearly 1,500 steel tanks, with a capacity of 60,000,000 barrels, furnish enough storage to fill a thousand ships. Through the pipe lines can pass, under high pressure, 750,000 barrels a day, although the average production for 1920 was about half of this amount.

In the Mexican fields in April, 1920, the latest date for which figures are available, there were 304 wells in production, 148 located and 123 drilling. The total of commercially unproductive wells to that date was 464, including only 35 which showed oil in too small quantities. Three-fifths of all the wells drilled in Mexico have been dry holes, and to-day of 1,113 wells drilled and projected, only 75 which have actually flowed oil have run out of production. These last, however, include some of the greatest in the history of the petroleum industry.

The vast investment and plant in the Tampico-Tuxpam fields produced in 1920 over 140,000,000 barrels of oil, one-fourth of all that was produced in the entire world, equaling some 40 per cent of the production of all the fields in the United States. The 1920 production was nearly five times that of 1913, when less than 26,000,000 barrels were extracted from the Mexican wells, and when Mexico's total oil output was only one-ninth that of the United States and contributed less than one-twelfth to the production of the world. The growth has been steady and by tremendous strides, for when the pressure of war was on, the men who were taking out Mexican oil built up a production which between 1916 and 1917 brought an increase of 40 per cent and began a development that despite superhuman difficulties gained such momentum that between 1919 and 1920 the increase was 60 per cent.

On your map you will easily find, on the eastern shore of Mexico, the city of Tampico, located in the center of the palm of the hand with which Mexico grasps the great Gulf. A little to the south you will find, with difficulty, the town of Tuxpam, midway between Tampico and Vera Cruz. From Tampico directly south to a few miles west of Tuxpam runs the "line" along which lies virtually all the oil yet developed in commercial quantities in Mexico. The "line" is thirty-five miles long; the great producing territory never extended over twenty miles; momentarily the section which is giving the oil of the Tuxpam district is along ten miles in the middle of the "line"—and the territory is hardly a half mile broad at its greatest width. This section produced in the past ten years 500,000,000 barrels of oil. In 1920 it produced about 140,000,000 barrels, close to one-quarter of all the oil taken from all the wells in the world.

Now trace the "line" north to Texas and Oklahoma—it is an extension of the great mid-continent field of the United States. Now go south, through the old Furbero field, swing a little in toward the Gulf, and south of Vera Cruz, on the Isthmus of Tehuantepec, you will find Minatitlan, the site of early drillings, and of the refinery of the Mexican Eagle Oil Company. Still south, on the "line," and you will find, if your map is large enough, the village of Macuspana, in the state of Tabasco. Here oil of a grade so fine that the natives burn the crude seepage in their lamps has been oozing through the soil for centuries, and here, long ago, the British drilled many test holes. The "line" runs true, skirting the Gulf of Mexico.

Still more. There are oil seepages on the West Coast, an extension, perhaps, of our California fields. Other indications have been found, even far inland, and indeed on the Gulf side, the "line" does not by any means cover the seepages, even of the coastal plain. All this section, off into the interior toward the states of Puebla and Hidalgo, has been leased for oil. But production sticks to the "line."

The Tuxpam field, the heart of the "line," will ultimately go to salt water. Of this there is no question. Every pool of oil that has been drained—now three in number—has given its 100,000,000 barrels, and the steaming, brackish water, still under terrific pressure, has wiped out the property, often between sunset and sunrise—a few hours between 50,000 barrels a day and nothing. Dos Bocas at the northernmost end of the "line," came in on July 4, 1906, hailed as the greatest well of history, blew out her casing, caught fire and burned for months, a torch of gas and flame 850 feet high, till (if it was oil and not gas she burned) she had easily spent her 100,000,000 barrels. Another great British well, Portrero del Llano No. 4, flowed eight years, giving nearly her 100,000,000 to industry, and went to salt water over night. The Casiano field, of the Doheny interests, paid a similar toll. Cerro Azul No. 4 of the same company came in at a full rate of 162,000 barrels a day. She has never been allowed to flow full, for the whole field is owned by the company, and the pool is considered safe from drainage. Further south, the Doheny companies have, in 1921, opened another vast field, the Chapapote Nuñez—but that, still, is "on the line."

During the past year the Naranjos field has been showing salt water; the Chinampa, with a hundred wells located on a relatively few acres, is being drained at top speed, and salt water has been cutting closer in at its edges. To-day the Zacamixtle camp, the last of the "line," which was drilled like mad by scores of crews putting down wells that cost in Mexico $100,000 each, has been narrowed to a strip of an oil river only a few hundred yards wide.

With Chinampa and Zacamixtle gone, only the Cerro Azul, the sixty square miles of the Chapapote field, and the adjacent Toteco pool will remain on the "line" with no reserves save to the south, in a territory recently proved by the "Toteco" and "Chapapote" districts, or to the north, in the Tampico or Panuco field proper. This last is a heavy oil section, and here, too, the largest portion of the territory is owned by the Doheny companies.

Why, with this dwindling field, this steady reduction in reserves, has there not been more development in Mexico? You know the basic answer—revolution. But through revolution and graft and theft and murder the American operators in the oil fields, working for British and American companies, have kept on the job. Revolution is not the only answer.

Carranza, when he became president of Mexico, cast envious eyes toward the oil fields, and sought to make them his own, for loot and for graft, and not for conservation, be it noted here. He "nationalized" petroleum, by his new constitution, and tried to force the companies to give up their properties. They did not surrender, in fact or in principle, and for five years have fought for their rights, and for what they believe is the hope of oil development in all the backward lands of the globe.

In 1919 Carranza stopped the drilling of new wells, in an effort to force the companies to submit to his decrees, and not until Tepetate and Juan Casiano went to salt water and the tax returns of nearly $30,000,000 a year (at that time) were direly threatened, did he give temporary permits for drilling. He might fight for the nationalization of the oil, but he was routed by the danger to the vast sum upon which he ran his government and upon which his generals and favorites fattened and grew rich.

Thus in the oil fields drilling has been resumed. But off the "line" there is virtually no drilling, none of the "wild-catting" which is the life of the oil industry. Until the new government, if it ever does of its own free will, loosens the death-grip of Carranza, the oil industry will remain paralyzed and confined to its narrow, shrinking bed between Tampico and Tuxpam.

But why does Mexico go on? Why does she see so little of the way before her? The situation is complicated by many factors, two of which stand out in relief. These are the support given the Carranza ideas first by the British companies and second by some new American companies. The British needs in Mexico have from time to time been identical with the American, and then the two have worked together, but the British occupy a peculiar position, going back to the Madero revolution of 1910-11. At that time the Mexican Eagle company (which is a Mexican corporation) was caught with a number of the old Diaz "reactionaries" as its company officials, and it was also the holder of the hated Diaz "concessions." As a result it had to walk the chalk line very carefully under both Madero and Carranza, a condition which has always made its position weaker than the American. The large local business of the Eagle Company, in refined gasoline and oils, as well as in fuel oil, has also complicated the matter. It was due to these and similar factors that the Eagle Company placed itself under the "protection" of the Carranza decrees when they were first issued, although with protests, both legal and diplomatic. With a single American exception, the English interests were the only ones which gave any comfort to those early Carranza plans. Upon their support the former president built many of his subsequent activities, including the ruling on drilling permits. He gave these permits to the Eagle Company without conditions, at the very time withholding them from the "unfriendly" Americans under a demand for a written waiver of all protest against future petroleum legislation.

The second form of support which the Mexican governments obtained is more recent, and more complicated. Under the Carranza decrees oil lands were open to "denouncement" (or filing of claims) and the taking out of a "denouncement" even to protect one's own property was taken as an unqualified recognition of the right of Mexico in confiscating the oil rights of that property. The American and British companies united in an agreement not to denounce their own lands and not to buy or lease denouncements upon any other lands.

In 1919, some new American interests, which had had other experience in oil, entered the Mexican field. They spent some $500,000 in looking up titles to the properties and leases held by the old companies. They found many defects, for the inheritance laws, the poor records and the negligible value of the properties as farm lands make questionable titles the commonplace of the oil game in Mexico. Where there was an apparently defective title, these interests acquired the outstanding lien, and so laid claim to some of the finest producing lots.

So far the plan was a not unexpected move toward getting a hand in the oil game, a chance to sit in with big stakes alongside the big companies. The new elements, however, next "denounced" their new claims before the Carranza government, thus placing themselves quite outside the old-crowd oil camp. This "denouncing" of their properties brought them many favors from Carranza officials, but it made negotiation with the old companies difficult.

The Mexican oil problem, in its simplest, is three-fold. It has to do, first, with the nationalization of the petroleum in the subsoil, which threatens to wipe out vested property; second, with the question of taxation, which may at any time, and indeed actually threatens to become confiscatory; third, with the problem of concessions which are to-day the most obvious form of political graft and to-morrow may precipitate a Mexican war over petroleum rights.

First, the nationalization of petroleum. The Constitution of 1917, adopted by Carranza, and continued by de la Huerta and Obregon, definitely declares petroleum the property of the nation. In the grants of land made by the Spanish crown (the basis of all land titles in Mexico to-day), gold, silver and other metals were especially reserved as the property of the king, and in colonial times and since have been worked only by special permission or grant under "denouncement," quite independently of the owner of the land. Neither coal nor oil was known to commerce in Spanish times, but in 1884, when the mining laws were revised, the Mexican government as inheritor of the rights of the Crown of Spain and retaining, as it did and does, the royal control over gold and silver, specifically stated that coal and oil belonged to the owner of the surface. This was confirmed later in the mining laws of 1892. In 1905, after oil was discovered and certain concessions for drilling had been issued to Sir Weetman Pearson (now Lord Cowdray), head of the Mexican Eagle Oil Company, an effort was made to have oil declared the property of the nation, like gold and silver, and thus subject to concession and denouncement. This was opposed by the American interests, which held no concessions. The issue was decided virtually unanimously by the Academy of Jurisprudence, and in the mining laws of 1909 the title to oil was definitely and unequivocably vested in the title to the surface soil.

Until 1917, the vast development of Mexican oil fields went on apace, based on the old property rights and apparently safe from molestation. Carranza switched the matter completely around by the simple expedient of adding oil to the list of minerals which are national property and placing the new ruling in that famous Article 27 which contains most of the anti-foreign provisions of the new constitution.

The Mexican defenses of this action are two. The primary thesis is that the subsoil has always belonged to the government, whether king or republic, and that it was beyond the power of ministers or courts or legislatures to alienate those rights. In other words, Mexico is only "taking back her own." The opposition to this is on the basis of vested rights, on the long periods during which the owners of the lands had actually enjoyed possession of the subsoil, paying taxes on full valuations, and on the virtual obligation of contract of all Mexican governments to support developments under the laws of their predecessors.

The other contention, more general and yet with a stronger appeal to modern radicals, was that such nationalization was in line with the trend of the times, a trend later manifested in the Russian revolution. Candido Aguilar, then Carranza's foreign minister, gave voice to this phase in his note of August 12, 1918, to the British Foreign Office, where he stated that "the modern conception of property is that it is a social function bound closely to the prosperity of the State."

Both these contentions might in fact be worthy of consideration if the government of Mexico were of a character to be trusted, if it were indeed genuinely devoted to any sincere ideals of social reform, if it were truly interested in the conservation of the nation's resources for the benefit of the people. But the Mexican governments have been none of these things, truly believe none of these things. The radicalism of Mexico, the socialism of Mexico, are means to an end, not ends in themselves, means to power and position, for loot and for the pelf which goes into private pockets and not even into national coffers.

Certainly if government could be depended on, the idea of paying fixed royalties to a national treasury is financially preferable to dickering with individuals, and obviously more businesslike. But since oil has been known, the great organizations which handle the product have been accustomed to dealing with private owners; it is a game they know, a business they understand. In Mexico there is the other factor which one can never lose sight of, and that is that government control means graft, favoritism, chicanery, the meddling of foreigners and big business in the very heart of the councils of government. And those things, until now avoided, must never come into being.

In the final analysis, the proposed nationalization of petroleum has never been a conservation measure, the only excuse (to radical or to conservative) for its promulgation. The Mexican governments, from Carranza to Obregon, accepted "denouncements" upon petroleum lands already developed, granted vast concessions for drilling, on a royalty arrangement with the government, in so-called navigable streams and other "federal zones," and in every way in their power carried on a *redistribution* of petroleum titles. This single fact of the government acceptance of such denouncements and concessions indicates that the intention is not to conserve, but to get a new deal with somebody besides the Gringoes and the Indians who own the oil lands sitting around the table.

The whole interpretation of the oil features of Article 27 seems at variance with the ideas of genuine radicals as completely as it is at variance with the ideas of dyed-in-the-wool conservatives who still dare talk of "vested rights." The effect of the enforcement of the nationalization plan would be first to change royalty payments from the land owners to the government and second to move the dealings for oil leases from the open field and the negotiations of plain buying and selling to the conferences of government officials where honor is to-day a more commercial commodity than land, and where the proportions of lease money to graft would be as one to ten. It would indeed, bring on the era of concessions and favoritism with a vengeance, and the dismal pictures of the foreigners' corruption and exploitation of Mexico would become a bitter reality.

At present, the chief hope of avoidance of such a condition lies in Article 14 of the same Constitution of 1917, which declares that none of the provisions of that instrument shall be construed as being retroactive. The interpretation of non-retroactivity has been the subject of much discussion. At one time Carranza's foreign minister told the oil companies that it should be understood to mean that the government would not collect for the oil already extracted. At other times it has been held that the expropriation of petroleum rights would not affect the properties where wells were opened prior to May 1st, 1917; then not to land acquired for drilling purposes before that date. It was this detail which was taken up by the Mexican Supreme Court in August, 1921. But after years of fighting single incidents, and working along the theory that American companies could demand only their own rights, the issue has actually broadened to the whole question of property rights of Mexicans as well as foreigners. There are millions of acres of potential petroleum land in Mexico, not one per cent of which is owned or leased by foreigners, and all this would be wiped out, along with foreign properties, if the oil were declared definitely confiscated to the nation, or even if merely the "oil" lands were exempted.

Were non-retroactivity interpreted to nationalize only the oil and coal in federal lands to which no title had ever been given to private individuals, the vested rights of land owners would be protected whether petroleum had been discovered on the property or not. Such an idea of nationalization would approximate the control of oil in national lands in the United States under the new leasing laws. It is this interpretation which the oil companies and the Mexican land owners are seeking, and which has not been touched by the Mexican Supreme Court decisions noted above.

The second issue in the oil controversy is taxation. Until the 1921 temporary increase, export duties on oil were collected at a theoretical rate of 15 per cent of its value. This valuation is supposedly on the basis of sales of oil in Mexico. There are hundreds of such sales, but their prices are not taken, and arbitrary estimates ostensibly based on the prices for which oil is sold abroad, less another arbitrary allowance for transportation, are the criteria. The results of this system have been confusing to the exporters, to say the least. Some of the lower grades of oil, for instance, were actually paying, not 15 per cent of their value, but 40 or 50 per cent. The valuations fluctuate also according to government caprice and the need of tax money; the result is another difficulty in making close prices to consumers, which in the end all must feel in the price of gasoline. A peculiar tax difficulty of the oil companies was over an exact doubling of the valuations and thus of the taxes, made by the Carranza government a few days before it fell—an increased tax which the de la Huerta and Obregon governments have sought to collect. Still more recent is the virtual doubling of oil taxes which shut in many of the wells during July, 1921.

The direct oil taxes are now about $2,000,000 a month, so that the doubling is an item of no small moment. At present no immediate solution of the tax difficulties is in sight, and the companies have been split by favoritism into two camps. One is largely British, which finds it profitable to accept the decrees. The other is largely American and finds the enforcement of the new regulations oppressive. Some plans for relief have been discussed. One of the proposed oil bills based on Article 27 interprets it not as nationalizing petroleum, but as nationalizing the right of taxation, taking all tax privileges from the states and vesting them in the federal power. The idea would be to provide a single direct tax on petroleum extracted from the soil instead of upon that exported. Apparently this tends toward a solution of the tax question. But here again enters the difficulty of dealing with Mexicans, for such a direct tax would be without recourse, until its provisions became confiscatory, while at present the companies have at least a chance of defense in protests against arbitrary valuations.

The outstanding fact in the tax situation, as in the nationalization question, is the bad faith of Mexican government. The much discussed reforms are non-existent, and government in Mexico is for the benefit, not of the governed, but of those who rule, and taxes fill not the treasury but the pockets of officials, and appropriations are not for schools and civic welfare, but for the army and "public works," where graft is so colossal that it passes the conception of citizens of simpler lands.

The third element of the Mexican oil problem has to do with concessions. This is a phase of nationalization, but to-day it has taken on an importance which recently obscured other issues. The government had issued a number of what are called "federal zone concessions," giving to individuals and companies the right to explore and extract oil from the rivers, lakes, etc. The federal zones are narrow strips along the seashore and navigable rivers on which an easement has been reserved for the public use. The American oil companies contend that this mere easement cannot be converted into absolute ownership, which is the effect when the government grants to third parties the right to drill wells there and thus to tap the pools of oil which the companies have discovered and developed and on which they are paying rentals to land owners.

There were a few oil concessions under Diaz, practically all to English companies. One of the great shibboleths of the Madero revolution was the wiping out of the system of concessions, so no more were given until toward the end of the Carranza régime. Beginning then, becoming almost an orgy in the brief rule of de la Huerta, and continuing into the days of Obregon, concessions have become common, some going indirectly to a few American companies, many to the British corporations and more to Mexican favorites of the ruling group. The concessions issued cover practically every river and semi-arid gully (regarded as a "navigable stream" for the purposes of the concession) in the whole Tampico-Tuxpam field, a stretching of the "federal zone" idea in order to make possible the penetration of the producing fields by concessionaires.

Other concessions are of different sort. Under de la Huerta one was issued giving the right to explore rivers, lakes and government lands over the entire republic, with preferential drilling rights up to a production of 400,000,000 barrels per year, the chief consideration being a return to the Mexican government of 40 per cent of the gross value of the oil found. Another, to a company, also American, gives rights to explore Lower California and other West Coast states, with the privilege of denouncing not only government lands, but private properties as well—the return to the government in this case is 10 per cent of the gross.

The concession feature of the oil question, like the others which I have described, has its rights and its wrongs, but the fact of giving concessions, and in such blanket form, to take oil from the lands of private property holders, is in itself proof of but one thing—the intention of the Mexican government, not to conserve its resources of oil for the benefit of its people and the generations yet unborn, but to get out of the oil business as much as possible as quickly as possible—and solely for itself and its favorites.

The final phase of the oil problem in particular and of the entire Mexican question in general is anti-foreignism. Article 27 of the new constitution contains a number of anti-foreign provisions other than petroleum nationalization. One is that only Mexican citizens may develop oil (and other properties) in the republic. Another section of the Constitution, as I have mentioned, gives this provision force by requiring that foreigners who sought to work such properties should appear before a government department and waive all rights of appeal to their home government for protection. This and other anti-foreign provisions are summed up in the so-called "Carranza Doctrine," one of the interesting developments of his picturesque reign. This has been stated as follows:

> "No individual should aspire to a better situation than that of the citizens of the country to which he goes; legislation should be general and abstain from distinctions on account of nationality. Neither the power of nations nor their diplomacy should serve for the protection of particular interests or to exert pressure upon the governments of weak peoples with the end of obtaining modifications of laws which are disagreeable to the subjects of a powerful country."

The world outside largely persists in taking Mexican professions at their face value, and in solemnly accepting the beautiful Mexican laws and the beautiful Mexican arguments as literally true. On this point I have quoted elsewhere the words of a great Mexican publicist, who has written: "The carpet baggers of Mexico have traditions rooted as far back as colonial times. They combine the shrewd and subtle wit of the Indian with the grandiose words of modern civilization, with which they have gained the sympathy of uninformed outsiders." Our own State Department has answered the "Carranza Doctrine" in no uncertain terms and once wrote that "the Department is of the opinion that ... an attempt is being made to coerce American companies ... to admit in advance ... the correctness of the contention of the Mexican government in the matter of ownership of oil deposits, against which the American government has made solemn protest as threatening confiscation of rights legally acquired by American citizens."

In fact, there is no reason to doubt that virtually all of the oil decrees of Carranza, all the rulings of his ministers, all the regulations which have been enforced with such insistence on petty details have been, first, appeals to sentimentalism abroad and, second, childish expedients to force recognition by the foreigners of some sort—any sort—of superiority in the Mexicans. In the last, so well set forth in the State Department message quoted just above, lies the basic cause of the failure of the companies to reach an agreement with the Mexican government. Every willingness to discuss a point, every slackening of their demands, has been accepted, not as an approach to a solution, but as a weak concession to Mexican "national pride" and personal dignity.

There are two remaining reasons why the oil question remains unsettled. They are extremely practical,—loot and incompetence. Of the former, George Agnew Chamberlain, the novelist, recently American Consul General in Mexico City, has written in his book, "Is Mexico Worth Saving?" that:

> "Today it is taken as a matter of course that ninety per cent of all Mexican officials in positions of trust are openly corrupt and will inevitably continue so until controlled by some greater power than any single faction of their peers.... The graft of Mexico is outright loot; its effect is to open simultaneously all the arteries of the body politic and to pour the entire life blood of the nation into the gullets of the group in power."

The oil companies are the ripest prey for loot in all Mexico. Their individual employees pay graft of certain kinds—of that I have no doubt, although there is vigorous and official denial. The companies themselves, however, pay a tribute, through the channels of astonishing taxation and contributions to public works, which is no less than the buying of the privilege of doing business. Another phase appears in the gossip which is general that one of the English companies materially aided the Obregon revolution—certainly every moneyed interest in Mexico had ample opportunity to do so. The American companies were, after Obregon's occupation of Mexico City, "shaken down" for about $1,000,000 which was credited against taxes—and the taxes afterwards proportionately increased!

As a whole, the companies have resisted the temptation to ease their way along the broader paths of high government by the voluntary use of money—they have generally confined their expenses to the ample totals of taxes and assessments. It is for this reason that one of the most serious phases of the Mexican congressional discussion of petroleum legislation is that practically every member of the Mexican congress expects "his," and when it is not forthcoming, will see to it that nothing favorable to the foreign companies finds its way to the statute books.

Lastly, incompetence. Perhaps the most appalling factor of the whole Mexican situation is the utter and profound ignorance of the men in control of the national affairs, men to whom the culture, the very procedure, of modern civilization are as a closed book. I believe that the oil problem is made serious chiefly because the Mexicans who might otherwise be willing to solve it are so uneducated, so limited in viewpoint and understanding, that they cannot conceive of the vast sums of money which must be invested in pipe lines, storage tanks, pumping stations, wharves and ships and refineries before the oil taken from their country's soil becomes the fabulous treasure of which they hear so much. They seem utterly incapable of grasping the fundamentals of their national problems; the pity of the condition almost obscures the significance of the fact. It has not been easy for me to explain the oil problem in its simplest phases to Americans, yet in this chapter you who have read it have learned more than the floor leaders of the Mexican congress will ever know.

It is through this forest of ignorance, this slime of graft, that the foreign oil companies are making their way. They have committed many mistakes in their handling of the situation, selfish mistakes, mistakes of ignorance, but the struggle has been against forces whose depravity has been literally unbelievable. Personally, I am no fire-eater, but I have seen much of Mexico and I have seen something of the psychology of depravity, and I believe that the last lingering hope of Mexican adaptability to world conditions lies in Mexican recognition of the need of grasping truth rather than theory, of facing facts with manly faith in Mexico and in Mexican ability to solve her problems as other nations solve theirs, by honesty and patriotism and not by graft and personalism. This attitude the oil companies have nurtured, and in this their policy has been a policy of weakness. Seeking here an outlet for the day, there a hope for the morrow, they have put a premium on Mexican dishonesty, given a prize for Mexican argumentative skill. I know some of the problems the companies have faced, I know the need for oil during the war, I have written here something of the magnificence of their achievement, but for all that, I hold that they have had much to do with the vacillation, the inefficiency, the watery, grafting policy of the Mexican governments from Carranza to Obregon. They have had a large part in making such a policy successful by not refusing unjust demands firmly and directly, by not challenging Carranza to close the oil fields, by not taking a mighty loss to save the endless leak of graft and taxes and cynical legislation which is their heritage to-day. Even yet their policy is one of conciliation to Obregon, the newest president; still they are offering compromise, still giving the subtle Mexican mind to understand that perhaps they might agree to Article 27, perhaps they might accept a little higher taxation, perhaps they would like a few concessions, perhaps they might be counted on to get the hopefully predicted Mexican loan.

All this is the last phase of the complicated problem. We have said, in days gone by, that this is the problem of the oil companies, that theirs is the gain and theirs should be the cost. But if I have succeeded here I have conveyed an idea of the breadth of the oil problem. It is no longer a question of whether the American State Department is making the proper moves to support honest and industrious American investors and workers abroad. It is no longer the academic problem of whether the oil companies are handling their business in an intelligent and efficient manner. The problem is ours, yours and mine, of you in Kansas, of me in New York, of our cousins in England and China. It is the problem of the chap who runs a Ford and of the man who is cutting our freight bills by renting us a truck, of the steamship company which is carrying our goods, of the captain of the battleship which keeps us safe from near and distant enemies.

The problem is not merely whether the white peoples of the world are to have the right to develop the riches of the backward nations for the benefit of the world, but of *how* they are to do it. So far, even in forward-looking lands, it has been impossible to eliminate private ownership and colossal private fortunes from the wheel of oil production; in Mexico, to-day, it would be disaster beyond understanding to turn the right of concession and oil privileges over to corrupt and inept government. The battle of the oil companies in Mexico is to save, first themselves from such a fate, and second to save all the unopened oil resources in the world from the strangling hold of such governments and such peoples everywhere. The oil industry can no longer carry the burden of such conditions, for the prices of your gasoline and your ship's fuel oil are reflections not of a world scarcity, but of the uncertainty, the colossal artificial difficulties of oil production in the backward lands.

Commerce has fashioned the world into one brotherhood, and the Great War, for all its appearances, has welded us all into a mightier machine of civilization than history has ever known. Oil is the fuel of that machine, and oil must come to its engine, though all the power of politicians and bandits combine to keep it in the soil. The backward countries are swept into the forefront of commercial importance when oil begins to flow from their soil. The process is going on all over the world. In Mexico it is at its zenith. The oil must come, and from Mexico before all others, for Mexico lies in the heart of the world, her shores touched by more waters in proportion to her area than any other continental nation. And her stores of oil are the greatest man has yet found or dreamed of.

To-day the world's need of oil threatens the life of Mexico. It is eating out her body by revolutions, by bandit governments, by colossal graft which feeds on the ever growing river of gold from the oil fields. The world's need for Mexico's oil threatens her with intervention, not because of capitalistic machinations, but because of the crass and wicked injustices which the wealth has tempted her to wreak upon her foreign residents, because wealth has undermined her government and given her over to demagogues.

CHAPTER IX
THE GOLDEN GEESE

In all these devious ways Mexico has tried to kill the goose which lays her golden eggs. Not the least onerous of her efforts in this direction has been the seeking she has always done to make the United States government and American business men take the responsibility for this precious goose of commerce. And sad to tell—to the Mexican mind at least—we have not always awakened quite promptly enough to our sudden new responsibilities, and the goose has more than once dropped near to dying in our arms.

That golden goose was the product of the nature of Mexico and of the régime of Porfirio Diaz. Long before Mexico became independent, long before the social problems which assail her now had been allowed to gain impetus, Nature had given up vast riches from the Mexican soil. Spain garnered them in, and gave Mexico such care as she knew how to give, and the golden era of the three centuries of Colonial life rolled out. Then came the first revolution, and the destruction of such wealth as Spain had left, until Diaz organized what remained and with it began his thirty years of peace.

In those thirty years. Mexico was changed from a land whose wealth poured out in bonanzas returning only caprice for industry and wealth for caprice, into one where industry, solidly invested capital, and wise foresight gained the golden fruit. In other words, the goose became domesticated, and produced golden eggs when she was appropriately fed with golden capital and golden brains.

It was literally the wealth imported and created by those years of peace and domestication which made possible the outbreak of revolutionary activity in 1910 and drove Diaz from Mexico in 1911. Prosperity was too much for poor Mexico.

The revolution, indeed, came at a moment of Mexico's saturation with prosperity. And it has continued by the continuation of that prosperity, which has furnished and still furnishes the fuel of banditry and revolution. It was not until after Diaz fell that the great wealth of Mexican oil became patent. And not until Carranza began imposing his taxes on the oil industry do we find the upsurgence of the ideas of socialism, bolshevism and nationalization which have been the battlecries of all the governments which have followed him. Oil, as we have seen, has furnished the sinews of war, and continues to furnish them, despite all that can be done to turn the tide.

In the days of the revolutions previous to Diaz the rewards of success were governorships, sometimes presidencies, and always some brief spell of peace. But to-day the reward is too vast, the graft quite too colossal, to slow down the round of struggle. Wealth pours into the national capital in amounts which would be quite hopeless of comprehension to the revolutionists of the older day. More tax money reaches Mexico City to-day from oil alone than Diaz had from every source at his command—while, save for the oil fields, Mexico is to-day a desert waste.

It is no wonder, then, that the nation can and does buy herself honors and praise in the world outside, that she considers it criminal that she cannot buy recognition, cannot force aid and trade and gold to flow to her. Is she not wealthy and can she not buy pages of advertising and the services of hundreds of propagandists of every type known to the trade? Gold is here and more gold she expects to bring to her through other channels than her own genuine advancement. She is back again in the days of the bonanza mines, when wealth went to caprice and labor and industry meant nothing.

And so she is killing the golden goose, just as she killed it long ago under the Spaniards, by forcing it to lay and lay and lay, till at the height of its productivity it is trembling to its death. Destructive legislation, the bitter threat of its confiscation, the continuing theft of vast sums in exchange for the privilege of struggling against these laws and threats—these are striking down the golden bird. To-day that goose is dying, and all Mexico seeks is to bring in, somehow, another goose to feed her hungry office-holders. She is willing that it shall be a relatively tame domestic goose, if only it will lay the golden eggs of foreign investment, trade, commerce—she would gladly go back to the relatively mild, but sure, wealth of the time of Diaz.

And what does she offer to induce that timid, wabbling goose across the national fence? I can see behind her promises of privilege nothing more substantial than outraged rights, and beside them, the panting, half-dead corpses of two golden geese of bonanza days—the almost dead mining industry, the sadly ill oil industry. For Mexico has limited mining by confiscatory taxation and by revolutionary outrages which left the mines in such a state that to-day the cost of operation is too great for them to continue under present prices. And she has set about the starvation of the oil industry, as we have seen, by limiting it to the narrow field of the Tampico-Tuxpam district, when the opportunities for oil development throughout the whole of Mexico are probably unequaled in any similar area in the world!

It is with such pictures as these that she would tempt trade and commerce and investment to Mexico. No, the "centennial expositions," the trade excursions, the special trips for special friends of the government, even the official telegrams of thanks to American officials who breathe a misplaced idealism with regard to Mexico—none of these, nor all of them, can quite make a screen before the unhappy corpses of the once lively golden geese of Mexican prosperity.

Let us resume, briefly, the list of the events which have marked the process of the years in the Mexican revolutions which began with the uprising of Madero—and which have been the means of killing foreign enterprise and native faith in Mexico's succeeding governments. The list is long, but it cannot be forgotten.

The revolution in 1917-1918 virtually wiped out religion in Mexico, profaned, sacked and burned churches, killed and outraged priests, violated nuns and girls in the convents, and drove into exile thousands of priests. The Constitution of 1917 virtually abolished religion, and yet the Protestant churches have been allowed to continue their work (with the result that many Protestant missionaries of Mexico were active Carranza and Obregon propagandists in this country). While most of the exiled Catholic clergy have now been allowed to return, they still work under conditions which make religion a virtual monopoly of the state, and practically eliminate religious freedom in Mexico.

Ten years of revolution have all but wiped out education in Mexico: first, by destroying the Catholic schools, which were almost the only educational system in the country outside the great cities, and, second, by so curtailing the appropriations for public school expenses as to make educational organization impossible.

The revolutionary hordes, when Mexico City was taken in 1915 by General (now President) Obregon, sacked the city almost as thoroughly as Attila sacked Rome, the public being invited by proclamation to join in the looting. Beautiful houses were made barracks for the soldiers; automobiles and horses, including those of foreign diplomats, were taken; stores and homes were broken open and robbed, and trainloads of rich furniture, including carloads of pianos, were shipped out, much of the loot coming to the United States to be sold. While the population, rich and poor, starved, no food was allowed to enter the city, and trainloads of beans and corn, the staples of Mexican food, were shipped out.

The revolution virtually suspended the political rights of the Mexican people. Under Carranza's decrees, which to this day form the chief basis of government in Mexico, no one may hold office who ever served under Diaz or Huerta, or who was not known to be a Carranzista before the Huerta uprising—save by special permission, granted only on personal appeal to the president himself. The revolutionists continuously refused to allow any Mexicans but those of known sympathies with themselves to participate in elections, so that only a fraction of the eligible voters have ever taken part in any election.

The revolution exiled from Mexico, on one pretext or another, virtually all the higher type of Mexicans, the men who throughout all Mexican history have been the stable and stabilizing element in the government, leaving Mexico in the hands of demagogues of the worst type, from the highest offices to the lowest. There has been talk of political amnesty, but none has yet been forthcoming, and the few Mexican exiles who return do so under personal assurance of their personal safety.

Mexico is to-day taxing her people, both natives and foreign corporations, to an extent and with a recklessness unknown even in war-ridden Europe. Taxes on imports and exports have been doubled and sextupled. The stamp tax has been quadrupled and broadened to cover almost every possible human activity; direct taxation on every form of industry and export taxes on the country's products have become the normal, where, before, these forms of taxation were distinctly avoided in order to encourage enterprise. Mexico is still spending more on her army, mostly in graft, than Diaz spent on his whole government, including interest on foreign indebtedness (which the revolution has never paid).

The present taxation system has been coupled with favoritism and graft to an extent that punishes with ruin any enterprise (save those fed from the natural resources of the soil, such as oil) which is engaged in a business where profiteering is not possible.

Carranza, as we have seen, financed his revolution by issuing 2,000,000,000 pesos of paper money, forced into circulation at the points of bayonets. None of this has ever been honestly redeemed. The paper money orgy covered three years, and absolutely wiped out all semblance of credit and all use of paper in business. In its course, the revolution took from the banks in "loans" approximately $28,000,000, completing the ruin of the banking system, as I have described above.

Carranza took over the railways of the republic in 1914, and since that date the revolutionary group has operated them for the profit of the government and themselves. They have increased passenger, freight and express rates to figures many times the normal, forcing the properties to yield the national treasury $1,500,000 a month, meanwhile paying nothing of rental to their owners, whose fixed charges are being defaulted at the rate of $1,000,000 a month—a total theft of nearly $400,000,000, growing at the rate of $1,000,000 a month.

The revolutionaries gained the support of the sincere Mexican progressives and of American students on the ground of a defense of the Mexican Constitution of 1857, but after they came to power they promulgated the Constitution of 1917, a new instrument, although the old Constitution was amply provided with means for its amendment. The new document is the most radical written Constitution in effect in the world to-day, but its provisions have been used so far only for the aggrandizement and enrichment of those who can abuse its privileges. The provisions for the confiscation and distribution of all pieces of land of large area have been used only to take properties of foreigners and Mexicans of the old régime to hand them over to revolutionary leaders. The provisions against the operating of mines, etc., by foreign companies have so far been used only to transfer such properties to friendly Mexicans and Germans. The provisions "nationalizing" oil deposits have been used only to exact towering taxes and millions of dollars of loot from the foreign companies and to drive the properties more and more into the hands of the British, Dutch and Germans, and away from the Americans.

The revolution has allowed and abetted the looting and ravaging of Mexico by every method known to brigandage. Hundreds of thousands of cattle have been killed for their hides; thousands of acres of standing crops have been wantonly ruined; seed grains have been stolen or destroyed; the vast sugar industry, left stagnant by Zapata's depredations has, since the government regained possession, been wiped out by the shipping away for "junk" of the machinery of the sugar mills; graft has been levied against relief trains sent by the American Red Cross to feed starving Mexicans and the contents of such trains even stolen and sold for personal profit of generals.

Carranza encouraged and abetted a military oligarchy which supported brigandage as a means for its own profit. Campaigns against the bandits and rebels were not pressed, arms and ammunition were sold by the federals to the bandits and rebels, in order that the military might continue to have work to do. The officers, acting as their own paymasters, padded the army rolls to many times their actual size, and the balance between the expenses and pay of the actual army and the phantom army was pocketed by the officers. The Obregon process, a variation of the Carranza plan, paid millions of pesos in cash and land to ex-bandits and revolutionaries, setting up Villa on a rich hacienda, and paying out the resources of the nation to buy the appearance of a peace.

Revolutionary favorites, as we have seen, were given the rich state of Yucatan for loot. They foisted upon that community (the only spot in Mexico where any wealth has ever been created through manufacturing and industry as opposed to the sacking of the riches of the soil), a so-called "socialistic" régime. A "modern state" was set up, and the experiment of taking from the rich for the benefit of the poor was set in full swing. By means of a great national monopoly of the hemp industry, prices were so inflated that in the course of five years the American farmer paid, in artificially-increased prices for twine for his wheat-binding machinery, $112,000,000 to the Mexican revolution. The state-controlled hemp trust has been forced to relinquish its control, and the costly experiment seems passed. Here is the first collapse of the Mexican fetish of socialistic demagogy, but it seems safe to believe that it will not be the last.

So stands the record, incomplete, shorn of detail, but each item taken from the history of shame which has been written in Mexico in the years just passed. Hidden behind a curtain of fair words and lofty idealism, the shame has been committed, but behind that same curtain to-day disintegration is hurrying on, coming as it came to Yucatan in the grist of inevitable retribution. That we may understand the end, it behooves us not to close our eyes to the beginnings.

The killing of the golden geese of recent years in Mexico carries a responsibility from which the United States cannot be entirely free. The eight years of the Wilson régime, when American foreign policy, as enunciated by Secretary of State Bryan, held that Americans who ventured abroad did so at their own risk and had no right to ask the protection of their government, was a mighty factor in the despoliation which followed in Mexico. Carranza, seeking the excuse for the policies to which the great wealth of the oil fields tempted him, found in this, our official attitude, his opportunity for baiting the Americans and with them most other foreigners in Mexico. His virtual espousal of the German cause in the Great War gave him still further opportunities, and the result has been written in the outrages which he committed against the Americans. This is a list only less appalling than the list of the outrages which were perpetrated against Mexico and the Mexicans in the name of the revolution. Here, briefly, is the record. Although many of its outrages were committed only during the Carranza régime, it must be remembered that that régime is the direct ancestor of those which have followed it, for the personalities seem the same, the shift in their places being the only change.

The revolution has killed over 3,000 foreigners, most of them in cold blood, probably not one per cent in fair and open battle.

The revolution has murdered over 600 Americans since 1910, and the revolutionaries have violated scores of American women.

The revolution has ruined over $1,000,000,000 worth of American property in Mexico through wanton destruction, cynical recklessness and savage bravado.

The revolution has driven from their homes in Mexico more than 30,000 Americans, men, women and children, who, in carrying to Mexico the high standards of American living, American business and American ethics, were pioneers of our trade and influence, and potential civilizers of Mexico.

The revolution has, as we know full well, promulgated that Constitution of 1917 which has been the bane of American, even more than it has of Mexican, business.

The Mexican revolution, by its baiting of the American government through nearly a decade, has nurtured in Mexico and sought to spread throughout Latin-America a hatred and fear of Americans and hostility to the Monroe Doctrine. This is threatening not only our own prestige on this continent, but the peace of the established governments of our Latin-American sisters, through the fomenting of hostility and unrest within their frontiers.

More than all, the revolution has made of Mexico a refuge for the enemies of the United States, first by allowing to be set up in its capital the central organization of the German spy and sabotage system in the Western world, and since the war by welcoming and aiding the bolshevists and radicals who are working openly for the overthrow of American institutions in this country and the destruction of American industry and trade in Mexico.

This is a bitter record, but without it, as I have had to say of many things in this book, the picture cannot come clear to our eyes. We cannot, in justice to our own understanding, forget that since the death of Madero, and even before, the Mexican revolution has been but one movement. The rulers who have succeeded each other have all been of the same group, and those in power in 1921 are those who were scrambling for place within the same ruling group in 1913. "The revolution," as one of them has said, "is the revolution." And so it is in more senses than one. We but deceive ourselves if in our very genuine desire to give each new Mexican president a chance, we close our eyes to the obvious facts of his political heritage and the human tools he must use.

Only one word more, and the tale of the golden geese is done. The protection which the American government has failed to give its traders and investors who have gone abroad has had an effect which those traders and investors must obviate before they step forth, at least into Mexico, again. Through the years of the Great War, our government, along with those of the Allies, put into effect in neutral countries, a "Black List" which was designed to keep German, Austrian and Turkish firms and their sympathizers from dealing and trading with the neutrals or with the peoples of the allied countries.

Mexico was of course our chief field for activity, and there our Black List had its severest test. In those months of struggle, we committed many faults; we shut off friendly firms from trade with this country; we encouraged, by many stupidities, the activities of smugglers and "cloaks" who bought for the Germans in Texas jobbing towns; we created for ourselves a phalanx of enemies of American trade who will not soon forget. Worse than this, even, when the war was over the tremendous machinery of the enforcement of the provisions of the Enemy Trading Act, with its literally priceless information regarding the business of Mexico, the capital and trade of the Germans, the Mexicans, and the Americans in the whole country—all this was thrown away. Literally it was cast into the waste-basket, and the information which if followed up and kept even partially up to date would to-day be the richest mine of information for American importers and exporters was scrapped like worn-out machinery. I do not know how many millions of dollars were spent in gathering this data for the War Trade Board, but I do know the nature of that data. It is gone, and the advantage which might have come from it is lost forever.

But the unfriendliness which was engendered by our mistakes, which was only slowly being wiped out by the correction of those mistakes when peace came—that unfriendliness remains. That is our only heritage of our Mexican activity in the war; it couples up with our own mistakes of ignorance or of carelessness during the same period.

From 1915 to 1919, literally all the foreign trade of Mexico passed through the United States. Imports and exports, the goods from and for England and Japan and China and Africa no less than our own domestic trade with Mexico went through the border ports by rail. Of necessity, the advantages of ship traffic were lost, and our manufacturers and our buyers of Mexico's raw materials had the greatest opportunity of all time to capture the vast bulk of the Mexican trade. The tremendous apparent increases in our Mexican trade during the war years were only the record of the world's commerce passing through our border towns. But to-day we have retained only a little of the gains recorded then, and we shall lose still more of what we have kept. And why? Because we have never truly sought Mexican trade and do not seek it to-day.

Ah, yes. We want to trade with Mexico, but, I repeat, we have never sought Mexican trade. We have wanted to sell Mexico our surplus, to have her take our extra runs and use the goods we have made in quantities for other countries. But we have never sought to meet the exigencies of the Mexican market. We have never done (as a nation, I mean, of course) what England and Germany have done; we do not follow specifications literally and send cloth, for instance, with exactly the number of threads per inch which the Mexican must have to get his best customs classification. We do not rearrange our patterns to meet a special demand of the Mexican market, carefully described to us by our customers. It is the old story of American trade everywhere in the world—our manufacturers have heard it in a dozen ways, and they are justly tired of the sound of it. My only point is that during the period of the war, when Mexican trade had of necessity to come to us in great volume, we did not link the Mexican buyer to us, either by meeting his demands or by helping him to understand our difficulties.

So it was that when the golden goose of Mexican business was surreptitiously put into our arms when we were busy with a lively war in Europe, we did not take the care of it that its parents might have expected of us.

The result is that to-day we have little hold on the trade of Mexico, despite the astonishing figures of our preponderance in it. For what we ship to Mexico is largely food and what we take from Mexico is largely oil—an exchange which is more significant than columns of figures in showing the economic condition of the land we trade with. Again we swing back to the one great, significant fact, the need of an activity which transcends mere barter, which has little to do with whether we are deceived by Mexican conditions or whether we are willing to risk them now for the sake of the great possible gains of the future. This is the issue of our duty to learn how we can serve in the solution of the problem—and to devote something of our energy to that solution.

CHAPTER X
THE HIGHWAY TO SOLUTION

The solution of the problems of Mexico's commerce and business seems to rest in hands alien to Mexico. The destructions of the past ten years are bringing her steadily nearer to annihilation, and Mexico herself seems helpless to save herself. These make the appearance, and it is vivid indeed. But it may still be only an appearance, if the forces which are acting and must act can be brought to see that they can and must work in Mexico herself.

The cycle of destructions insists upon showing itself as the round from the materialism of Diaz on to the destructions of an era of profaned utopian idealism and now to an era of materialism again. But this time it is an era of materialism which differs from the Diaz time, and is more potent, at the moment, for good and for ill. For to-day, in the high places of government, controlling through their greed the very minions of government, is an animating power which is not the idealism nor the self-sacrifice of devoted rulers, but the worship of wealth alone. That power is mighty for destruction, but at the very moment that it functions thus, another form of wealth, "capitalism" if you will, is working slowly for the saving of such of Mexico as is being saved. For "capitalism," in foreign guise, in such enterprises as even the mad radicals of the day point to as the signs of their "progress"—here capitalism is giving Mexico her only surcease from the destructions of her rulers.

Wealth is the one power which men recognize in Mexico. It is to-day above government, for it dominates government and destroys government by the very temptation which it holds out to successful revolution. It rules to-day in Yucatan, even as it ruins the individuals of Yucatan. Yet, too, it rules in the oil fields, for it makes the vast production of oil possible, because it alone has the power and the foresight to develop oil's potentialities. And there, in the oil fields, it is being turned, ever so slightly, to the beginnings of its ultimate destiny, which must be, I believe, the saving of Mexico.

Strange tales I have told of the oil fields, and yet it is a far stranger tale which I have now to tell. For I would point out the vast opportunity which awaits that wealth of oil for the saving of Mexico. In the light of that possibility, the mighty stream of oil which in a thousand ships pours from Mexico into the industries of the globe, is a helpless Niagara, childishly unconscious of its own power.

The constitutions and laws and decrees of the Mexican revolutionaries still hold the wealth of oil in their grip. There has been, in the summer months of 1921, a mild effort to break that grip, to stay the hand of strangulation which is at the throat of the oil industry, but this is still self-defense. There is a yet more persistent force than mere taxation or even than mere confiscation at work in the oil fields of Mexico. This force savors of elements mightier than mere industry; it seems to be taking the form of a sinister elaboration of the vital principles of bolshevism—the bolshevism which rules in Russia and is a battle cry in Mexico.

Among these principles of bolshevism, enunciated by Lenin himself a year ago, was the setting of the capitalistic powers at each other's throats, such powers as Japan and America, that they might destroy one another.

In Mexico we see that threat from Russia developed with the thoroughness of a too-eager pupil. In Yucatan the cycle has brought two vast financial interests to battle—the millions of the Equitable and the Royal Bank of Canada, against the International Harvester with other unlimited resources. In mightier and more daring terms, and even more deliberately, in Tampico and in the false issues of concessions, Mexico and the governments, radical, bolshevist indeed, of the revolutionary era, have been setting not merely groups of financiers but the interests of nations at each other's throats. The issues of concessions on the one side and open oil fields on the other seem to have been planned and fomented and distributed with a deliberation which is not Mexican to bring the United States and England to grips—in Mexico. So the spoken threat of Lenin finds elaborate action in distant Mexico.

Oil has been the victim, the tool, then, of those who would destroy our civilization? We do not know. But this we do know—that to save itself, to save great nations from war, to save the world's oil for the uses of civilization, oil must come to its own rescue. It may be saved temporarily in other ways than by itself, but itself it must save sooner or later. If sooner, the power will be for good; if later, it will be for destruction, even as the powers in Yucatan are being expended for destruction. The comparison is inadequate, perhaps unfair, but the vision is crystal clear. It shows the last great power of the world—wealth—diverted from its proper channels to battle within itself. The dragon's teeth of capitalism have raised up armies and the stone cast by bolshevism has thrown them at each other's throats.

And this cannot be, and must not be. Our civilization rocks. Were it to pass on to the millennium, the rocking would be worth the price. But we see, not the millennium, but, as in Yucatan, the coming of new destructions, with capital, and labor, in rôles of ignominy.

For to-day oil, and the capitalism it represents, as yet does little good for Mexico. It pours its wealth—nearly $50,000,000 a year—into the coffers of government and there, like the golden apple, it creates discord and wars and bloodshed. It feeds and fattens the group in power and makes it worth the while for other groups as fast as their petty agitations will allow, to rise up and overthrow their predecessors, to the end of getting their share of the loot, and a new distribution of favors. The gold which pours into the national treasury inspires, as we have seen, all manner of radical legislation and constitutional provisions and oppressions to make the capitalism which develops the oil disgorge more and more of oil's wealth, and bow more deeply beneath the yoke of political personalism.

Thus is the gold which flows from the oil wells dynamically active—as a poison and a weapon against those who create it. The oil companies of themselves take no part in Mexican politics. This, I admit, is almost unbelievable, but I am convinced that except where government—our government or that of England—has directed them, the oil companies have not used their power politically. The United States and England have both taken hands in Mexican politics, and particularly was Washington active in arbitrating the destinies of Mexico in the eight years just closed. But that does not concern us just now. The liquid gold from the oil fields has never used its power alone.

It has not yet used its power for its great possible good, either. Not even for so much good as the International Harvester and the Eric corporation have used theirs in Yucatan to the discomfiture of Alvarado and the chastening of the henequen industry. Never, for the sake of a principle alone, has an oily hand been lifted to say "thus far and no farther." Never has an oil official done more than cry aloud over the pressure of the thumb-screws—cries which do no more than extract more wealth to fatten the generals who, with added strength, only gave the screw another turn.

For seven years the oil companies paid the rebel general, Manuel Pelaez, a comfortable tribute. In that time they also paid Carranza all he asked in "taxes." They were helpless, and the war was the excuse, not for strength on their part, but for submission to unwarranted and unjust oppression, oppression which had no object save personal aggrandizement and enrichment.

Here is the one power in Mexico which is potent, accepting the rule of corrupt government, passing on its power of gold to those who use it for nothing but their own ends, and for the destruction of all that our civilization holds dear.

They buy privilege in Mexico, the privilege to do the business which they must do, while the sinister powers to whom they pay tribute cut them from the development of new fields upon which their ultimate future and Mexico's immediate future depend. The whole power of Mexican revolution and of the groups which control the revolution lies in that one principle which I have reiterated: they give no rights, they sell no rights; only privilege is on the auction-block. Those who buy it to-day and those who contemplate the buying of it as a way to enter a promising foreign trade and investment field are the upholders of the shameful exploitation under which Mexico herself bows. And of these, the greater sinner, to my mind, is he who plans to enter Mexico now. After all, we must in fairness admit that the old companies have the potent excuse of their vast holdings and of their duty to their stockholders.

The plan which I hold as the solution of the economic and political chaos of Mexico would comprise a shifting of the center of control from politics to economics, where the motive force, at least, has ever rested. I would no longer tolerate the application of political remedies for economic ills, but would go so far as to suggest an economic remedy for both economic and political afflictions. Apparently this is what our government plans, and what Mexico's government will not bring herself to accept.

Years of observation of the Mexican problem has led to the conviction that the international difficulties of Mexico are between the Mexican politicians and the American government—their interests decidedly conflict. But there is no division of interest between Mexican business men and American business men; the former are just as disturbed over the confiscatory policies of the Constitution of 1917 as are the latter. So recently as April 7, 1921, a petition was sent to President Obregon by a group of landowners in the Mexican state of Jalisco, protesting against the enforcement of the rulings of the "National Agrarian Commission" which confiscated their properties in the name of the "social revolution" under the same Article 27 which attacks foreign property rights. Its words are worth recording as an indication that it is not alone the American business man who feels the pinch of the rule of privilege in Mexico.

> "Such commissions," the petition reads, "are nothing more than partisan centers where laws, reason and justice are mocked.
>
> "This atrocious work will be judged by public opinion as soon as the deep and serious damage which has been done is known, and history will in time establish the responsibility. Suffice it to say that in every case it has been a work of destruction and never of construction....
>
> "The local agrarian commission is inventing fantastic plans of taxation, confiscating large and small properties, and sugar, *mezcal* and orange plantations, which have cost their legitimate owners years of toil and the investment of considerable capital. The federal tribunals, deaf to all appeals, follow an invariable line of conduct in every case against the landowners. Should the landowner invoke in his behalf the same doctrines which have been applied to the benefit of others, he finds out that these same doctrines are never interpreted in his favor. The authorities only favor those they wish to favor and to accomplish this end they do not hesitate to override justice and reason."

It is to this Mexican business man, still a stable factor in Mexico, that we must look for the change in government attitude toward business which is indispensable to the solution of the social, economic and political chaos of Mexico to-day. In numbers these Mexican business men are few; in grasp of world affairs they lag behind men in similar positions in this country. Nevertheless, their interests, those of the American companies now operating in Mexico and those of the Americans and other foreigners who hope to share in Mexican trade, are and will be one. It is in the way of supporting such Mexicans in their efforts to influence the government of their own country that I speak of an economic remedy for all the afflictions of Mexico. I would, if I could, put them in control, would bring back to their aid the brains and the energy of the exiles who belong, in one way or another, to their class of producers.

It is to such an end that the foreign business man who hopes, in the immediate or in the distant future, to share in Mexican trade should turn his hand. He should demand, in the councils of his government, in the congress of the country, in the powerful conventions of chambers of commerce, that Washington insist definitely on a return to civilized and economic rule in Mexico. This Washington seems to seek but they and they alone have the power to compel the decision by the powers of this world that the day of privilege in Mexico must be put aside, and the era of equal rights shall dawn. In the hands of American business interests the tool of pressure is very powerful. This is a moment, not to rush in to get easy markets on the "ground floor," but to demand conditions which will give the opportunities and the profits to those who can best use them—the truly Golden Rule of business the world around.

When that day comes, all will profit. Until that day comes, none can have aught but risk and chance, the chance of the gambler. For who can say how the wheel of politics will turn? And only he who knows Mexico and the Mexicans of old can assume that he can buy his way to privilege with the next pirate crew. The solution is in the hands of American business men because it is in the hands of the Mexican business men whom they can support and aid. And in the group of such Mexican business men we must include not only the true Mexicans, but the foreign companies which have worked long in Mexico and so have made themselves a true part of Mexico, vitally concerned in her progress and prosperity.

Those foreign companies of Mexico are the business world of Mexico. And they know Mexico and her needs better, in many ways, than Mexico knows herself. They know, as every one who is honest with himself knows, that the hope of Mexico is in truly devoted, native government. Yet we still see them pass the power which could to-morrow restore Mexico to the family of nations over to those who use it for their own ends and for the utter destruction of all Mexico that is outside the influence of the oil fields and of their civilization.

The great companies are Mexican, in essence. They have rights as Americans and as Englishmen, to be sure, but their greater right is in Mexico. And they have the right to use their power as they will. They seek to be good and to be honest and just, but the ends of justice are defeated by their very honesty. I do not advocate activity in politics, nor even the tangible aid of oil companies to revolutionists of any stamp. I hold only that if the oil companies would give over their profits (as they did temporarily in the summer of 1921) long enough to shut off the stream of gold from corrupt government, if they would thus render revolution and loot unprofitable, the solution of the problem of Mexico would soon come, in a return to an age of honest work and honest government, free from the temptation of vast unearned wealth. We need not ask how or by whom the change shall be made, whether by a sincere Mexican government ready to cast out its evil elements, or by a government yet to be born. That is not our concern, for our concern is to search for our part and having found that part, to play it well.

Is not this a solution of the Mexican problem? Should we not say to the foreign companies:

"You are in Mexico, you are of Mexico. You represent all that is stable in Mexico. You know those Mexicans who can solve the country's problems, and make Mexico again a land where white men can keep the altar fires burning bright, where honest Mexicans, and foreigners if they will, may help to make it all that it should and must be."

Revolutionary radicalism has run its course in Mexico, and we are back again at a rule of capitalism, a rule which capitalism, for right or wrong, cannot longer avoid. The eyes of the world are on the moneyed powers of the world. It is childish to try to deceive radicals or conservatives with saying anything else. To-day, in Yucatan, capitalism (because circumstances have forced it to do so) is exacting the toll of penalty from the henequen industry and its native spokesmen. To-day in Tampico, capitalism hesitates to move on, and waits for the ruin which will tumble about it, forcing it, in its turn, to grind Mexico beneath its heel. Somehow, dimly, seems to emerge the lesson which Mexico has for us and for the world. Capitalism must in the end save the world from the ruin of revolution. To-day in Mexico it can move quickly and freely. To-morrow it may be clutched in the very destruction which is upon it, and be forced, itself, to the destruction not alone of the enemies of our civilization, but of the fabric of progress of that civilization. The story of Yucatan is written. Is the story of Tampico and all

Mexico to follow the same plot, and is the world to go blindly on, believing that in compromise it shall gain strength?

Truly the crimson feast is preparing for the vultures, and vultures will our eagles of business become if they wait longer on their distant heights for revolution to finish its bloody orgy. To-day there is yet time. In Mexico there is yet time. Why wait for the chaos, from which there seems but one emergence, the emergence to intervention and blood and long foreign rule? The one stable force, the wealth of Mexico, must choose a nobler course than that waiting, than that cynical hoping. It can choose and it must choose. Old worlds are indeed passed away and the paths of new stars are to-day being plotted. In the courses of those new stars power will be used without apology, as the revolutionary radicalism which our old civilization created moves without apology. Our duty is to the future, not to the dead past of compromise and convention and self-righteousness. Is capitalism honest and sincere and bound up with the welfare of the human race? Or is it indeed the vulture which waits to feast only upon dead bodies amid ruins? To-day in Mexico it waits vulture-like. Its sincerity and its true righteousness are to be determined not by slavish waiting for the ruin which will force it to use its power, as it is using it in Yucatan, but by its moving, to-day, to the solving of the great problems of a great nation as it alone can solve them. Capitalism and not revolution, the corporations and people of Mexico, and not foreign pressure, must in the end give answer before the last Tribunal.